Evil at the Heart of Capitalism
Daniel Miles in conversation with Karl Gruber

We live alienated in a world made hostile by the 1% of
people possessed of the wealth and power required to
marshal events in accordance with their will. And their will
resolves ever more earnestly to pursue the exploitation of
the 99% of ordinary people who are put to the service of
this richest 1%. The profits, the bonuses, and the extrava-
gant living of this parasitical 1% are extracted from the
efforts of the 99%, whose standard of living has remained
static for over 30 years, whilst the 1% carries on heedless of
environmental destruction and the growing threat of
climate change. If we want a future that is worth living in,
in which we can exercise our own autonomy, we need less
work, not more, less exploitation of both human resources
and those of the natural world, and an abandonment of the
obsession with economic growth, in favour of well-being
and quality of life. The first step is to realise that we are all
enthralled to the diktats of the 1% who, in their positions
of power and authority, make happen exactly what they
want to make happen. The next step is to broadcast this
message. What comes after that *will be down to us.*

In their stimulating discussions, recorded throughout
2012, Daniel Miles and Karl Gruber examine a set of simple
beliefs that need to gain currency if the evil of capitalism
is ever to be effectively challenged.

Evil

at the heart of

Capitalism

Daniel Miles

In Conversation with Karl Gruber

Typeset in Guardian TextEgyptian 9.5/15 pt

To contact the authors, please tweet Daniel Miles
@vigilantecarer, or find us at his blog
http://scroungersrevenge.blogspot.co.uk

ISBN 978-1-291-91482-5

'Of the hearts that daily break,
    Of the tears that hourly fall,
Of the many, many troubles of life,
    That grieve this earthly ball—
Disease and Hunger, and Pain, and Want,
    But now I dreamt of them all!

✳   ✳   ✳   ✳   ✳

'The wounds I might have heal'd!
    The human sorrow and smart!
And yet it never was in my soul
    To play so ill a part:
But evil is wrought by want of Thought,
    As well as want of Heart!'

Two verses from *The Lady's Dream*
by Thomas Hood (1799-1845)

No society can surely be flourishing and happy, of which the far greater part of the members are poor and miserable.

ADAM SMITH

OCCUPY

Contents

Introduction

Crisis walks the earth.

From the subprime mortgage fiasco in the United States to youth unemployment in Greece, from near global financial collapse in 2008 to revolutionary uprising in Tunisia, Libya and Egypt, from record-breaking extreme weather on almost every continent, to war in Syria; and everywhere strife, austerity, inequality, lotteries, the crassness of reality TV and the cruel sham of social mobility.

The mantra of this age seems to consist of but one word, frequently uttered, tacked on to virtually all known nouns, meaningless in its ubiquity, if not causing impotence then laughing at it. The mantra is **CRISIS** ... banking crisis, unemployment crisis, immigration crisis, energy crisis, food crisis, water crisis, Euro crisis, humanitarian crisis, housing crisis, economic crisis, debt crisis, ecological crisis. You name it, and it is probably in some sort of crisis. You'd think human beings have completely lost the plot, that everything is running out of control and no one has a clue what to do about it. The poor queue up outside food banks, and the rich hide themselves away inside their gated communities watching on their TVs the queues outside the food banks.

Well, excuse us for thinking this is just bonkers. Excuse us for wanting to know what bunch of idiots have broken human history, and are about to break the planet itself. Excuse us for declaring the stark, staring obvious, that there is something grotesque and vile, something truly evil grinding away underneath all these crises. We gaze upon it, and we will give it a name. It holds us all captive to the destruction of everything, and we will name it. Like a boot stamping on our faces forever,[1] we will name it. And by this name will our enemy be known: *capitalism*.

Everything has its cause, for everything there is a reason why it has come to be like that, and for everything there is an explanation. This book is our explanation for today's stupid mantra.

I first encountered my good friend Daniel Miles at secondary school, here in the UK, in the late 60s, when spirits were high and the future promised so much; though, as we have travelled further from our youth, our enthusiasm for the future has dwindled in proportion to the distance travelled. After school, while Daniel went to university to study philosophy, I tasted army life for a while, though through it all I never abandoned my intellectual interests. He taught his subject to new students for a few years (though veered into

---

[1] With apologies to George Orwell and this quote from his novel *Nineteen Eighty-Four*: 'If you want a picture of the future, imagine a boot stamping on a human face - forever.'

the life of a full-time carer[2] before the age of 40), and after a long and circuitous journey, I found my vocation as a Christian minister. In fits and starts, we stayed in touch, sometimes with news, but often with none. As most of us do, we struggled with our commitments and pursued our interests as best we may. But always we endured a sort of disillusionment, a frustration not with our own lives, but a frustration with the context in which we were trying to live them, a frustration that focused ever more keenly on the society which as well as sustaining us, also - in certain ways - abused us and took advantage of our intentions to mean well.

Our discontent, ever present, disquieting yet not properly analysed, forced us to make a serious assessment when, in the summer of 2011 as we watched on our TVs the rioters vent their fury on the streets of UK cities, we realised that their anger and our exasperation, their desire for vengeance and our despair flowed from the same source. It was time to make a response to the pain and frustration and irritation and resentment that the System had been heaping on us. We had had enough: we had all had enough.

Destruction, to be sure, is a terrible thing, wasteful and likely harmful, something we could not join in with nor encourage. Yet on the telephone to Daniel on 8 August as we watched the furniture store *House of Reeves* in Croydon engulfed in flames, we knew something had changed. For here was a message that came from us as much as it came from

---

[2] A carer in American English is a caregiver or a caretaker. (Though a caretaker in British English is a janitor...)

the people in the streets, as much as it came from 33-year-old Gordon Thompson who set the blaze and who would stand trial for his actions.[3] We had had enough. We could no longer tolerate the sheer nastiness, the crassness, the mean and bigoted hypocrisy of the society we wished so much to contribute to in meaningful ways, but which kept slapping us in the face. For those in power, those with power, those listed with the other 1% of the population who make happen in this world exactly what they want to make happen, were laughing at us, living the high life at our expense, bullying us and taking advantage of us - of all of us who number amongst the 99% they have got to work for their comfort.

How do we stop this madness? And before we got very far with our ideas on how to do it, we saw that others were already doing it, or at least making the attempt. On 17 September 2011 we watched as 5,000 Americans, inspired by the *indignados* movement in Spain, descended on Lower Manhattan, waving signs and beating drums, with their slogan, *We are the 99%*, vowing to occupy Wall Street and 'bring justice to the bankers',[4] their occupation of Zuccotti Park hailed by some as America's Tahrir Square.[5]

That's what we need here in the UK, and everywhere: an uprising, a revolution. Next came Occupy London (which

---

[3] See this at the BBC < bbc.in/1jGSbZd > where you will find video footage of the fire, and hear an interview with the owner of the shop.
[4] *Wikipedia* 'Occupy Wall Street' article < bit.ly/1lqcWeH >
[5] Referring to the plaza in Cairo where protesters were campaigning for the removal of Egypt's President Hosni Mubarak as part of a much wider movement across north Africa and the Middle East calling for freedom from tyranny, described as the Arab Spring < ti.me/NegVNn >

like Occupy Wall Street, had intended to locate its protest in the occupation of a major financial district, but had to settle instead on the precinct outside St Paul's Cathedral).[6] And in their number we saw for the first time the masks based on that worn by 'V' in the *V for Vendetta* film of 2006,[7] worn by people declaring themselves to be *Anonymous*. For it was not *who* they were that mattered, but *what they believed*. Towards the end of the film when the corrupt policeman who has been pursuing 'V' fails to kill him, despite firing his gun at him repeatedly, says, *Why won't you die?* 'V' replies, *Beneath this mask there is more than flesh. Beneath this mask there is an idea ... and ideas are bulletproof.*

And this is where we have located our own small contribution to the uprising - in ideas, and in the beliefs and value judgements that underpin them. In short we have tried to understand the source of our own outrage at events and our revulsion for the ugliness of the human world in terms of understanding - in terms of understanding the ideas by which we interpret the world, and the ideas by which the 1% oppress us. Our task here is to explore and communicate these ideas and bring them to consciousness.

The conversations that follow are all based on tape recordings made between December 2011 and January 2013. During the spring and summer of 2013, as time allowed, we edited, and sometimes extensively rewrote, our discussions in the hope of arriving at clear, simple, and hopefully interesting texts that might guide and inspire readers to find

---

[6] *Wikipedia* 'Occupy London' article < bit.ly/1lqcDR4 >
[7] *Wikipedia* 'V for Vendetta' article < bit.ly/1kyZFgD >

those personal insights and convictions about what actions will serve best to promote the global revolution that this planet so desperately needs.

Our sincerest hope is that our discussions may help others find a clearer understanding, find confidence in the principles they adopt, and find an enthusiasm for communicating their insights, but also find opportunities for putting those principles into practice and help them contribute to making the world a better place.

KARL GRUBER
30 September 2013

1

Brass Tacks

KARL GRUBER: *Given the sheer range and the severity of the problems that are produced by all the crises that I mentioned in my Introduction, does this amount to capitalism itself being in crisis?*

DANIEL MILES: No. This is what is so strange about the situation today. For the people whom capitalism serves, the billionaires and millionaires, for the 1% identified by the Occupy Wall Street movement, *there is no crisis for them*. They are benefiting from what is happening. They are accruing for themselves ever more power and ever more wealth. For them, capitalism is working perfectly. It's exactly as they want it.[8]

---

[8] See for instance, Taylor (2013, 52), who writes: 'This is not a time of capitalism in crisis, but capitalism in the full throes of its joyous existence.' He remarks on the same page that 'the primary goals of neoliberalism are the continued production and accumulation of capital by a tiny elite'. No sooner had the Conservative-led coalition been elected to power in May 2010 that the new government set about reducing income tax for those who earn more than £150,000 a year, whilst Prime Minister David Cameron kicked ordinary people in the

And for the rest of us, the pain just goes on getting worse.

Well, the situation really is intolerable. The statistics one reads in the papers are staggering, almost unbelievable. Anyone can look them up for themselves. Of course, we live in Britain, and our immediate awareness necessarily focuses in the first instance, on events happening here, in our own country. But the trends we see here are pretty much common across the whole of the western world, in Europe and the USA especially. As I say, the statistics are staggering. For example, the need for food banks is expanding enormously.[9] Youth unemployment is at record levels, and here in Britain, zero-hours contracts, which force workers to make themselves available at any time, but without any guarantee of any work, are on the increase, impoverishing ordinary people and at the same time enriching the wealthy.

If you could name one thing at whose door we can lay the blame for today's global crisis, what would that be?

Exploitation. In two key senses. First, we have exploitation of the environment, not just in the sense of making use of what the natural world has to offer - as when a team from a hunter-gatherer group sets off to hunt an antelope, or the

---

teeth with his utterly fatuous remark: 'There is no "them" and "us" - there is us. We are all in this together, and we will mend our broken society - together.' *Conservative Party* website <bit.ly/pGdxhe>
[9] See the *Wikipedia* 'Food Bank' article < bit.ly/1eyHzLt > and this at the *Trussell Trust* < bit.ly/1cYpJgM >

earliest farmers sowed their first crops - but something today more serious, more sinister, more destructive, something only ever seen, if at all, hitherto on very local scales (I can think of Easter Island, as an example of that point), but which in our modern industrial era is undertaken on an industrial scale, with its processes, procedures, methods - call them what you will - which set out to extract at a maximum rate the bounty that our world can make available to us. No matter what the cost, no matter that in going about it this way, the capacity of the planet to go on providing this bounty is curtailed or, with respect to some sorts of produce, even ended and denied to all future generations. This is the sort of exploitation which environmentalists are concerned with, and if we can we would like to contribute to an understanding of the mentality, insanity, if you prefer, that motivates this planet-wide ruination.

But secondly, we must address what can be called human exploitation. This is the misuse of power by which the person who wields the power has such control over other people (one, a few, or maybe many) that they bend them to their will, such that in making other people work - make things, grow things, clean things, design things - gather up for themselves as much as possible of the proceeds that the work creates. In other words, they keep the profit.

You are referring to the basic operation of capitalism?

Just so. The system under which capitalism works has become the elephant in the room that no one dares speak about or speak against, or put another way, capitalism is now the only game in town, and its seeming inevitability cannot be questioned. Its dominance continues to be supported not only by those few who benefit from its persisting (in our new age of frustration, referred to as the 1%), but also, it seems, by many (the 99%) who are in fact its victims.[10]

But this too, considered separately from the question of the evil of ecological destruction, is also something evil, something that demeans us and shames us. It really is as simple as that. Understanding it and exposing it, and then standing against it and demanding an alternative way of living is an essential process that must be championed if human beings, in the end, are going to live in a dignified way on a planet that is no longer being systematically plundered to provide gargantuan riches for the few, and meagre, demeaning crumbs for the many.

Where, then, shall we begin?

We will begin by asserting one key proposition - that exploitation of the individual and of the environment is in a deeply

---

[10] Writer Fredric Jameson in his essay 'Future City' (2003) reminds us that someone once said that 'it is easier to imagine the end of the world than it is to imagine the end of capitalism' (see also Žižek 2011, 334); and this attitude, that there is no alternative to capitalism, is referred to as 'capitalist realism' by Mark Fisher (2009). It is of course to the advantage of the rich elite who benefit from maintaining the operation of capitalism just as it is, that we believe in this utter absurdity of capitalist realism. Well, we don't believe it, and we don't want our readers to believe it, and by the time they have finished reading this book, we hope that they won't.

fundamental sense, both the driving force that makes capitalism possible, and at the same time it is the fountainhead
of the most profound evil that threatens everyone. As individuals, we are threatened at every turn: as students,
workers, members of families, as sick and disabled people,
as carers, as pensioners; we count for nothing if we do not
submit ourselves to the creation of profit appropriated by
the wealthy. Our personal aspirations for creativity, love,
learning, fulfilment, meaning, are allowed only to the extent
that our efforts make the wealthy wealthier. Our aspirations
are allowed only as inconsequential side-effects - they certainly are not regarded as core values that when denied deny
us something that is essential for human life, something
essential for us that relieves what otherwise must be lives of
miserable drudgery and fruitless endeavour - to be of benefit
only as the producers of profit for the few whom fortune has
cast as our masters.

Raise your hand if you think we should have our lives
dictated to by masters.

**An imbalance
between rich and
poor is the
oldest and most
fatal ailment of
all republics.**

– Plutarch (46 - 120 CE)

OCCUPY

2

Capitalist Exploitation

KARL GRUBER: *The exploitation we suffer is not like that which we may witness from afar, as when we watch a TV show like* Cowboy Builders, *or even experience as the individual who through sheer happenstance ends up ripped off by a cowboy builder. That sort of exploitation occurs against a background of general non-exploitation, the world of decent builders where rotten apples are few, and where sooner or later they are dealt with by Trading Standards, the courts, or indeed by a TV show like* Cowboy Builders.

DANIEL MILES: Though, we should be careful not to throw out of our account the attitude that the cowboy builder has to his victim, the person whom he regards *not as a person* with feelings and rights and difficulties, someone who is doing their best to live a decent life, but merely *as a resource to exploit* for his own benefit. This attitude, that people have an entitlement, when they are able, to take advantage of others, in exactly the sense that they may take advantage of any resource, whatever its nature, is central to our contention that at the heart of our capitalist System there is the most profound evil - the use, through violence or the threat of violence or through some sort of intimidation, of other people as a mere resource for the benefit of those who happen to have the wealth and the power to successfully pursue that objective.

That this attitude underpins, or rather provides the completely robust and seemingly indestructible foundation on which stands the whole capitalist edifice, does not mean that those who own businesses dependent on the profits that they extract from their workforce themselves possess that attitude. Surely we can find any number of well-run businesses, owned and managed by perfectly decent people?

I am sure that is right (perhaps not as sure as you, though). There is a tension between attitudes that individuals have, on the one hand, and the attitudes that are - what shall we say? - embodied in the System itself. It is as if we want to say that only occasionally do drivers take positive delight in the destruction of the hydrocarbon molecules that occurs when they drive their cars. Some drivers, to be sure, do not even know that this destruction is taking place. Yet whether they know it or not, the destruction occurs. It is the same with the capitalist System.

The System (I think we should use a capital 'S' for 'System') has formalised, made normal, made inevitable, made compulsory, made ubiquitous, a new sort of Slavery under which our lives have objective value only to the extent that we satisfy the requirements of our Master, who will have at any cost what he wants.

This is simply a matter of observing what is actually going on. Capitalism has established a SYSTEM of relationships and practices within which the rich elite at the top (the 1%, in contemporary parlance) possess an all-encompassing POWER through which they maintain their position of MASTER over everyone else lower down the scale of wealth (the 99%) asserting their POWER disproportionately over the poorest, whose labour they put to use, making of such people nothing more than an asset or resource to exploit for their own benefit.

To these MASTERS we are all answerable and ultimately beholden (because they control absolutely the story of how and why this world comes to be the way it is). We are the PRECARIAT enslaved to their SYSTEM.

But people, the 99%, wouldn't willingly put themselves in a position to be so easily abused.

The trick is so clever, so simple, so in-your-face, so deviously malicious that we will have to spell it out. This truth is so nasty that it deserves to be left in the schoolyard, in the hands of the bully, where he tries to carve out his petty empire of fear by beating up anyone who inadvertently wanders too close to his orbit, and who gets sucked in for a pummelling, or gets spat in the face, or gets a tirade of crude, essentially incoherent abuse screamed into their wincing eyes. Yet the nasty deceit of capitalism, far from staying isolated in the schoolyard, subsumes the whole globe into its empire of abuse. All human activity joins together to form one vast machine whose sole output is profit for the rich;

and woe betide anyone vexed by concerns over environmental issues, or global warming, or, God forbid, the rights of workers to dignity or decency or a living wage.

The trick is simple. This is it. Its full glory is revealed in a pathetically simple, if not simplistic, imaginary example. (Real cases may be substituted whenever you wish.)

Imagine a small umbrella business. It is owned by one person who employs five people to run the operation - to work the machines, do the accounts, manage the stock and dispatch the orders. Each worker is paid the same: £400 per week (approximately £20,000 per year). The wages bill, for one week, is therefore £2,000. Imagine that all the other costs - raw materials, electricity, rent, cleaning, maintenance, shipping charges, etcetera - come to £8,000 per week. For this business to be viable, it must gross £10,000 per week. Let us imagine that the business does well, and sells enough umbrellas to gross £20,000 per week. The owner therefore takes £10,000 per week for his own pocket, making his annual income approximately half a million pounds. Twenty-five times that of his workers.

The gap between what the business needs to break even and what it actually makes is the profit.

Indeed so. But notice what has actually happened. If the workers went home at lunch-time on Wednesday, having completed half the working week and having made half the number of umbrellas, the business would make £10,000, its break-even figure, and all would be fine, and each worker can take home their £400 weekly wage.

If the owner is to get a pay-packet the same size as his workers (presuming that he does actually contribute to the business in some practical way), they may need to work another hour-and-a-half, or so.

That can be accommodated. The point is, that all those extra hours worked beyond the break-even figure do not result in any benefit for the workers, but solely and exclusively for the owner. In terms of the bare logic of what is happening, the workers are giving the owner half of their time, which they are compelled to spend labouring in his business, *for absolutely no benefit to themselves.* The evil we wish to point to in these conversations is found in the transactions of a society, our society, where this abusive relationship is embraced as being perfectly acceptable; and where the accomplishment of the owner and his dazzling entrepreneurship is praised to the sky as if he has done something worthy of challenging the gods. Yet the workers are condemned as troublemakers, agitators, perhaps as communists, if they raise questions about a living wage, about being treated decently, about deserving a share of the profits that they created in the first place.

3

Evil and its Varieties

KARL GRUBER: *In order to understand how the capitalist System causes or promotes evil for those people who have no choice but to carry on living under its dominion, we should investigate the nature of evil in its own right.*

DANIEL MILES: The notion of evil permits a demarcation between lesser harms and misfortunes, and those that are more, or significantly more, severe. The loss of a toothbrush hardly counts as a misfortune, even if the frustration of its loss is experienced as an irritating inconvenience. Whereas, in contrast, the community that suffers the loss of its annual harvest has surely suffered an evil, and the degree to which its members starve, and perhaps even die as a consequence of the loss, determines how severe this evil is.

And the severity of the evil is marked by how much pain and suffering it causes, for how long that suffering is endured, whether it is attended by temporary or permanent physical injury and disability, but most importantly for our discussion, whether it results from someone's intentional action.

But this points to two separate sources for evil. You mention both a natural phenomenon, such as a storm or a flood that destroys a community's harvest, but also the intentional actions of a person that results in the suffering of others.

Of primary consideration, I think, is the suffering of the person who is subjected to evil. If we imagine two people rushed to the same hospital on the same occasion, one whose legs have been seriously injured in a terrorist attack, and another who was not able to get out of the way of a falling tree who also has serious leg injuries, our immediate concern is for *them*, our hope to be able to relieve their pain and distress, and whether there are treatments whose application will result in full or worthwhile recovery. The evil they have suffered causes immediate pain, but also threatens them in other ways. Are these injuries life-threatening? Will I walk again? Will I be able to keep working? What will happen to my family? We are able to ask these questions easily and instantly from the position of the injured people. We have a very good idea how that evil would affect *us*. This capacity for empathy is perhaps the most essential component of being human. (As I think we will show, the prevalence to which the capitalist System both ignores and undermines this capacity is the fountainhead from which flows some of the worst evil on our planet.)

So on the one hand, we have natural evils, devastating storms, the falling of trees, and so on, which have no connection to human agency, and on the other hand we have what we can call moral evil - the pain and suffering caused by the deliber-

ate actions of human beings (the terrorist, in your example). It is the latter, moral evil, upon which we mean to focus our discussion? And in particular, the actions that result from the workings of the capitalist System?

Just so. But we must keep alert to the ways in which the effects of natural evils may be made worse by the injection of moral evil. One clear example of this is the disaster in New Orleans caused by Hurricane Katrina in 2005. Had all those people whose responsibility it was to build and maintain the levee system done their jobs properly, if those agencies had fulfilled their functions at federal, state and local levels, possibly not a single death would have occurred. And perhaps the individuals, families and communities, who suffered the devastation of such 'natural' destruction, would have suffered less, recovered more quickly, and found solace in the thought that all that should have been done had in fact been done.

Many other examples can be found where greed, corruption, or some other failing that counts as moral evil has allowed the awful effects of natural evil to ruin lives or kill people, when otherwise the awful effects would have been prevented or made less severe. The example comes to mind of poorly constructed buildings collapsing when they should not have, when shaken by a minor earthquake, all because officials and construction companies set aside their responsibilities in order to line their own pockets: such people do not just steal money that should have been spent on properly constructed buildings, but they also steal the lives of the people crushed under their moral failings. The folly and pain and suffering of moral evil are not infrequently amplified by its (not always inadvertent, but certainly culpable) use and direction of natural evils.

Perhaps the most striking and most potentially devastating example we can point to today is the reality of global warming. The lust for power, the greed for wealth, and headlong desire for 'progress' purchased through the wholesale destruction of traditional ways, has directed human history onto a catastrophic course towards destruction. I have the impression that many people think, because the coming devastation will result from the effects of natural phenomena (rising sea-levels, desertification, acidification of the oceans, epidemics and pandemics, and so on), then that is not so bad. That is like thinking that if an epidemic were to be caused by the foolish or selfish action of some person or corporation, then the deaths that result would be viewed as less awful than if people had toured around neighbourhoods putting bullets at random through the heads of exactly the same number of individuals.

And of course the denial of climate change, championed by those representing and promoting the interests of the corporations that cause it, provides the very basis on which to all the more earnestly pursue the practices that cause climate change...

One important observation, I think, is the idea that depriving people of their needs is a moral evil; that is, evil is not just the presence of bad things (seas that inundate, trees that fall, harvests that fail, buildings that collapse), but is also, in some circumstances, the absence of good things. The work of the twentieth-century humanistic psychologist Abraham Maslow is immensely helpful in this regard.

Indeed it is. Maslow's breakthrough came when he realised that any study of human psychological pathology would be incomplete if psychologists were to study only those people who have mental health problems. To understand what has gone wrong for such people, we need also to study those people who are most healthy. Instead of studying only what is wrong with ill people, we need also to study what is present and normal for people at the other end of the scale, who enjoy very good health. We need to understand bad health in terms of the absence of good health.

I think we should introduce a diagram at this point, to illustrate Maslow's 'Hierarchy of Needs'.

We should point out that Maslow's original account allowed only for five levels in the hierarchy, and originally the top four levels in our diagram were included by Maslow under the inclusive heading 'Self-Actualisation'. Later commentators felt the need to explicitly expand the diagram into the more clearly definable content that Maslow discusses.

Maslow's interest concerns human motivation; why it is that people do what they do? The first four levels of need at the base of the pyramid can be considered *deficit needs*. When the objects of these needs are lacking, the person who does not have them is motivated to acquire them. This is obviously so with respect to the lowest of physiological needs, which are required merely in virtue of the biological facts

TRANSCENDENCE NEEDS
helping others to achieve self-actualisation.

SELF-ACTUALISATION NEEDS
realising personal potential, self-fulfillment, seeking personal growth and peak experiences.

AESTHETIC NEEDS
appreciation and search for beauty, balance, form, etc.

COGNITIVE NEEDS
knowledge, meaning, self-awareness, etc.

ESTEEM NEEDS
achievement, status, responsibility, reputation, etc.

BELONGINGNESS AND LOVE NEEDS
family, affection, relationships, work group, etc.

SAFETY NEEDS
protection, security, order, law, limits, stability, etc.

BIOLOGICAL AND PHYSIOLOGICAL NEEDS
basic life needs – air, food, drink, shelter, warmth, sex, sleep, etc.

Figure 1

Abraham Maslow's Hierarchy of Needs

Although Maslow did not himself in any of his writings represent the Hierarchy of Needs in this pyramid form to describe these levels, it nevertheless seems appropriate to portray the notion of hierarchy in this format, and many commentators have done so.

that determine how human bodies function. Failure to satisfy these needs will mean death, sooner or later. And the lack of these needs obviously constitutes an evil for the person who endures their absence. At best, privations of these needs inevitably results in discomfort, if not downright suffering. The evil of hunger, when at first all it causes is discomfort, is not unendurable for most people. Yet, after a short span of time, what earlier was merely a hardship is now life-threatening. In common with all animals, human beings are programmed by instinct to seek remedies for these basic privations.

The source for the deprivation of these basic biological needs, as we noted earlier, may be on the one hand natural, and may be on the other moral, when through folly or meanness or the intent of hateful actions, one person by acting immorally deprives another of the bare essentials of life.

To what extent should we really accept Maslow's Hierarchy of Needs being reflected in a genuine hierarchy in real life? I mean, it seems perfectly possible that a homeless person on the streets can gain tremendous spiritual enrichment from the beauty of nature, as they study a tree in autumn, ablaze with yellow and red leaves, say, or steal a book of poetry, and find themselves transported by the English Romantics.

Maslow accepts that, probably for everyone, needs are only ever partially fulfilled.[11] Of course, the needs at the most basic, physiological, level are essential for life and for even

---

[11] See Maslow 1943, 386-8.

the most basic standard of good health. And although everyone must surely wish that all their safety needs be met to
reasonably high standards, it remains a fact of life for almost
everyone that total security is not practically possible. What
is possible becomes more and more precarious, or at least
more demanding for its satisfaction, the higher up the hierarchy we move. Only a few are blessed with perfect mar-
riages, say, and probably only a minority of people can ever
say that theirs was the perfect job which fulfilled them completely, and fewer still will wish to acknowledge that their
transcendental needs have been satisfied.

But there is a sound and obvious observation to make
about this Hierarchy of Needs, and that is that for anyone, it
is better to live that life in which these needs are met, rather
than not met, and the degree to which a larger proportion of
needs are met is the degree to which that life is more desirable than possible alternatives.

We may hope that all people have some insight into what
makes a life more choice-worthy than any other alternative -
what we would like to be true of our own lives, rather than
untrue.

*Though I fear many people view this in terms of money alone,
that the greater one's income, one's wealth and possessions,
the closer to the ideal of happiness and fulfilment one must
necessarily approach.*

And those who think this for some time are surely disabused
of such a simple perception, in the end, when they find
wealth alone does not of its own accord bring fulfilment. We

must hope so. But the System we are objecting to continually fails to realise this truth, that wealth may be a means to support a way of life that is fulfilling, but can never in itself constitute such fulfilment.

Two essential points arise from Maslow's observations. First, the truly desirable life that it is rational to choose for oneself is the life containing the greater quantity of satisfied needs, and that this is a fact about the nature of human beings that no political or economic system could ever hope to change, but must recognise only in the sense that the leading of fulfilled lives may be encouraged and supported, or may be thwarted and denied. Secondly, that the System under which we are compelled to live, the System which purposefully sets out to exploit us in the service of the rich, necessarily destroys not only the possibility for maximum fulfilment, but often blocks access to even the most basic needs, and denies us the autonomy of making those choices from which fulfilment may be deemed most likely to follow. The System is in fact destructive of human nature, and therefore destructive of our very selves. That this destruction is purposeful makes it evil, something to condemn and resist - something with respect to which we have a duty to enlighten others - something with respect to which we must rise up with the utmost indignation.

That things should have come to such a pass is not acceptable.

At the very moment we realise what has come to pass, we say 'no'. We say 'no' with a swollen sense of abhorrence commensurate with the evil we see perpetrated by the 1% who administer the System for their own advantage.

4

Slavery in Our Time

KARL GRUBER: *I would like to pick you up on a couple of things you said in Chapter 2. You remarked that the way the capitalist System exploits us in effect* enslaves *us, and that it* enslaves us to a single, vast machine *which creates profit for the wealthy plutocrats who operate it [bottom of page 23]. I am interested to know how you think these terms should be taken. Are you using them as metaphors, or is their use here mere hyperbole?*

DANIEL MILES: Of course, exaggeration and extreme emphasis are most definitely intended, because they are needed. The situation is so dire that emphasis must be the order of the day. You cannot rage without emphasis. Rage without extremes of expression and behaviour remains just an internal dialogue, in which you acknowledge this un-wanted, horrible frustration and fury. What sort of indigna-tion can be acknowledged, let alone expressed, by merely recognising as fact a certain level of dissatisfaction, after which you just go to make a cup of coffee? How can it make sense to do something about making a coffee, but leave one's frustration to fester unattended? So, at least sometimes, we must stop everything and express our rage. And, as you explained, the purpose of our discussions is to awaken a new consciousness in which this rage, and what provokes it, is properly understood.

How does that relate to your mention of slavery and a 'Profit Machine' [in the last Chapter, last line of page 23]?

Well, 'slavery' especially is a strong term, so of course I mean it hyperbolically: it is a term not normally used. So yes, it exaggerates something, and it questions how we should think about it. It flags something up. It works like a discord in music, or like someone using an air-horn in a context where its use is not expected. But I also mean it literally. There is a real sense in which 99% of the world's population, treated as a resource to exploit, really are unwillingly and unwittingly (perhaps) put to work with the sole purpose of serving the interests of the richest 1%. So, yes, we are slaves, pretty much in the usual sense of that word.

But I would like to start by first explaining my use of the expression *machine* - and your reference to a *Profit Machine* reflects exactly what I had in mind.

So people are working in a machine, or servicing a machine - or they are the machine?

Obviously, there is a tension here between simile or metaphor on the one hand, and literal meaning on the other. When we ordinarily think of 'machine', we think of a bicycle, or a sewing-machine, or a lathe in a factory, or all those machines lined up on an assembly-line that in sequence, step by step, put a car together. The thing that makes the welding sparks fly, that's the archetypal machine. But consider the factory [in which these machines are located] *as a whole*, as one giant machine into which at one end go raw materials and unassembled parts made elsewhere, and out of which at the other end come finished cars (say). This super-machine is made up of more than just the individual machines contained within it.

For there is another, *biological*, machine superimposed on the factory-machine, and this comprises all the movements and interactions of the people who work in the factory. Without their activity, the mechanical factory of metal machines is useless, it can't do anything. The people move things about, they work the controls, they repair the machines, they top them up with oil, or ink, or glue, or raw materials.

This human machine must work with a certain precision and accuracy that rivals any mechanical device, or the holistic combination, people-in-the-factory, would function poorly, or not at all.

But the thought I would like people to ponder is this. The human machine does not stop at this particular factory. The individual members of this biological machine, a machine made of people and their bodies and all their activities, interact *outside* this factory.

They have homes to go to, interactions with their families, children to take to school, food to buy and prepare - a whole range of activities. This is what characterises human society.

Indeed. But what we have here is one vast and complicated *biological machine*, as I want to call it, which overlaps and superimposes its activities on factories and offices, all workplaces, whose primary purpose in the economic hegemony of our times is the creation of profit for the rich. We are all functioning components in the *Profit Machine* that is superimposed over almost the entire land mass of this planet. For the economic hegemony, we exist solely for the purpose of fulfilling our role within this machine. Anything else that might matter to us, our families, our poetry, our art, our personal fulfilment, is *entirely irrelevant*. Indeed, those who manage the Profit Machine for their own benefit would rather that we did not have such aspirations. They are a nuisance to them, because having them, we are not wholly dedicated to the enterprise of serving the System. They are tolerated, and wherever possible exploited, to the degree that we serve the System as consumers.

And this picture, this reality of people functioning as components of the Profit Machine, is a picture of a people enslaved?

Yes. We have already explained [in Chapter 2] the brute arithmetical facts about exploitation, when we imagined the specific example of the umbrella factory.

But let's imagine something on a much grander perspective. Let us imagine a city, any city, anywhere. And one morning, in our imaginations, we fly over the city as if we were birds, swooping and darting in any direction we please, glancing through any window, any doorway, learning the truth, and hastening on.

And what is this truth? It is the simplest thing, but in seeing it, our insight might be profound. We see people doing
things. We see them getting out of their beds, changing
nightwear for other clothes; we see them eating and drinking to sustain their bodies. We see many of them moving
their bodies around, here and there, within their dwellings,
and then outside in the streets. Some of them make use of
transportation devices. Some of them walk. They go to other
locations.

Put aside for the moment all abstract notions. Put aside
work and *wage*, and *teacher*, and *welder*; put aside *father,
mother, van driver*. Put aside any *transaction, money, debt,
promise*. Put aside *drudgery, hope, anxiety, despair*. Keep
them ready, but do not yet admit them. They may wait. For
now, we gaze upon what is real. What is really there. The
brute facts concerning the things that are really in the world.

*You mean this as a thought-experiment? Perhaps we should
imagine ourselves not as birds, but as aliens from another
world who have come to study human culture, and this is our
first day of making observations.*

Yes, I like that idea. At this preliminary stage, we simply do
not know how human culture works. All we can see are the
observable, purely physical manifestations of what everyone
is doing. And that's all there is. *People doing things.* Eating
and drinking, well that is easy to understand. But more con-
fusing is our observing the exchange of some sort of token,
paper or little discs of metal, that occur either before or after
the food is consumed. Most puzzling are the rectangular

plastic cards, which are either handed over, then handed back, or inserted temporarily into some device, or sometimes just moved across its surface. What is odd, is that these rituals with the paper, bits of metal, and plastic cards seem not to occur when people consume nourishment in their own dwellings.

But, by goodness, do we see this busy race of funny looking, apparently sentient, hominids *doing things*. Many go to dedicated 'doing-places', where they do things. They work machines, they *make* the machines, they fit together, glue and weld, sometimes take apart. Others are doing things at communication devices, peering at data on displays and responding to what they find there by tapping on tapping devices, whilst others are talking into devices they strap to their heads or hold in their hands, apparently in response to messages or queries or instructions spoken by others in distant places. Then there are 'places-for-the-young', where older ones talk a lot, and the young ones write things down, or perform basic scientific experiments; then outside, some of them run about, and even jump over rods erected horizontally, it seems, especially for the purpose. Others remain in their dwellings, especially those who care for very young ones, though we see instances where these very young ones are taken to 'places-for-the-very-young'. And there are also 'places-for-the-sick' and 'places-for-the-old'. But everywhere *doing things*.

Some of these doings, we may be sure, are important or even essential for the effective running of human society, for growing food, for making garments, for the construction of dwellings, and the care of the sick. Other activities seem to fall into other categories. The 'place-where-they-hit-the-balls', using long, fine staves, where some celebrate the little white ball arriving in a little hole from which sprouts another staff, sporting a little flag at its upper end - this place seems not to have any significance for the growing of crops or the repairing of machines. We are confident now that some of the human doings are in fact games, undertaken for amusement alone.

But now we are starting to reintroduce abstract ideas into our account.

We are. But of course, a full and proper understanding of how human beings live cannot permanently leave out of the account these abstract notions, though to what extent alien researchers could ever approach a complete understanding is another question.

How does this relate to the claim that people working as components of the Profit Machine are rightly regarded as slaves? For 'slave' is also an abstract concept...

Let us imagine that the aliens, having studied for a while a modern city - London, say - can go back in time and study an ancient city.

Ancient Rome would be an obvious choice...

Yes, let's make it ancient Rome. And the obvious and striking difference between modern London and ancient

Rome is the lack of technology. Modern London is stuffed with technology, with pipes and wiring, machines of all kinds, the Underground, cars and buses of course, and the whole city is awash with the microwave signals of mobile phone traffic. Not to mention computers and broadband and satellites in orbit overhead.

All that is simply missing from ancient Rome.

All of it. Not invented yet, the aliens will realise. But when it comes to the brute facts about *what the human beings are doing* - well, *there is no appreciable difference*. From the point of view of the doings of the people, allowing for the absence of modern technology, the two cities are exactly similar. Yet, what the aliens have yet to fathom, is that in ancient Rome, almost all the productive work required for maintaining the life of the city is undertaken by slaves. From cooking to digging sewers, manufacture in workshops to the construction of buildings and pavements; from making clothes to cleaning them, from loading and unloading and guiding the wagons in between - if not all of it, then almost all of it is done by slaves. Even caring for and educating children was in many instances turned over to domestic slaves.

But who are the intended beneficiaries of all this arduous endeavour? Those at the top, the slave-owners, the wealthy, those in power and those with power.

The 1%.

The 1% then, and the 1% now. The doings by which the 1% are maintained, maintained in their wealth, in their power, in their luxury, is exactly the same. But notice the trick that has been played upon the mass of today's working people who work *as slaves* without the slightest idea that they *are slaves*.

In ancient Rome, the 1% could take ownership of what the labour of their slaves produced only by *actually owning their slaves*. They had to take physical possession and control of the people who worked for their benefit. And that meant they had to provide accommodation, clothes and food, however meagre, and to be sure, sometimes, medical care. A healthy slave, especially one trained in sought-after skills, did not come cheap. In the city at least, as opposed to the rural, agricultural setting, I think I once read in the book of some scholar many years ago, that such a slave in the ancient world had a value comparable to the price of a modest car in the modern world.[12] That means that when your slave falls ill, you do not hesitate to call in a doctor, just as today, the car owner gets their car fixed if it starts to make a funny noise. Indeed, you look after them to a jolly decent standard.

---

[12] See the article 'servus, servitus' ('slave, slavery') from
< bit.ly/dDobhu > William Smith, *A Dictionary of Greek and Roman Antiquities* (London: John Murray 1875), and search for 'price' to find his analysis on the monetary value of slaves. His prices in UK pounds sterling for 1875 may be converted to today's prices at the Measuring Worth website < bit.ly/1hWQDbt > A brief survey of websites discussing the Atlantic slave trade from the 16th to the 19th centuries suggests a very similar range of values.

I think I remember hearing that modern research found that different sectors of the ancient population in Roman Pompeii, slaves and their owners, consumed exactly the same diet.[13]

Well, there you are then. And here is the trick. Those who labour, who are exploited, for the benefit of the 1% must today care for themselves! They must find and maintain their accommodation, must buy their own food, buy their own clothes. They must even pay their own water bills! *In this regard* at least, working people today are treated worse than the slaves of ancient Rome. And good God, does not the indignity of this weigh us down? As wages and social security benefits fall in real terms, and as the cost of living keeps rising, the capacity of the 99% to successfully care for themselves diminishes day by day.

But the key difference between the slaves of the ancient world and the 99% today, is surely the fact of personal freedom, of not actually being owned by anyone as an item of chattel.

Maybe that is so. But maybe what the difference amounts to is smaller than we might think. In both cases, the value that the working person generates through their labour is appropriated by their owner (in the case of a slave) or employer (in the case of a worker), and the cost of living is handed back in the other direction, in the form of food and clothes and so forth (for a slave) or wages (for a worker). In both cases, the

---

[13] For rich and poor eating the same diet in Pompeii, see this at the BBC website < bbc.in/f2UFMk >

slave as well as the worker are directed by some sort of management structure. The slave may be ordered about by their
owner, just as the worker may be ordered about by their employer - or both may receive instruction through some management structure manned by other slaves or workers. The
differences are minimal. The similarities are astounding.

But I return to my point about the slave not actually being free.

I think we should be very careful in assessing what this
'personal freedom' enjoyed by the modern working person
really comes to. To be sure, we can imagine the slave in ancient Rome preferring to swap their life for that of a working
person living in today's world. But I am sure there would be
many ancient slaves who would not want to swap, because
they would view their situation in ancient Rome as prefera-
ble to that of the modern, exploited worker. Of course, as I
say, both worker and slave are exploited. Both Systems -
slavery and wage labour - have been designed to take away
from the 99% of the population a substantial proportion of
what their labour produces, to be enjoyed as something stolen by the wealthy and privileged 1%; and as I say, *what
these people actually do*, how their labour manifests in the
physical world of making and cleaning and so on and so
forth, *is fundamentally the same.*

Let us bring back those abstract qualities we earlier set
aside to conduct our thought experiment. Let us bring back
drudgery, desperation, exhaustion, humiliation, helpless-
ness, melancholy. But where should we apportion them? To
the slave or to the wage labourer? To the person exploited in

the past, or the person exploited today? And how can 'freedom' alleviate the horrors of exploitation? When is today's worker free to set a fair wage? What is freedom that must clock-in at set times or face sanctions? What is freedom when one's lavatory break is timed? What is freedom to the zero-hours contract worker who must report for duty at the behest of a text message, or lose their job? How worthy of the name is this freedom that must submit itself to the humiliation of claiming welfare benefits because you are paid less than a living wage?

What is freedom when you work for the luxury of others? How can such a miserable situation find a remedy?

We may start by learning that 'freedom' in today's global economy means freedom for the 1% who enjoy riches and power to hire and fire as they please, to shut down production here, and start it again in another country where they can pay a fraction of the wages they were paying before. To enjoy their freedom, they put 99% of the world's people in servitude.

And perhaps we are free to aspire to social mobility, to rise above the other suckers, and hope that although we sense something despicable in this attitude that I myself may be saved when everyone else must drown, we can promote ourselves out of exploitation and into the ranks of the exploiters.

5

The Cruelty of Social Mobility

KARL GRUBER: *In November 2006 in an interview with the* New York Times, *Warren E. Buffett, one the world's richest multi-billionaires, remarked 'There's class warfare, all right, but it's my class, the rich class, that's making war, and we're winning.'[14] That suggests on his part, not just a perception that the richest 1% in the world are exploiting the other 99% as a resource whose labour creates the wealth that the 1% heap into their bursting pockets, but an attitude that the 99% should be regarded in a particular way, as prisoners of war, as booty, as slaves, as serfs whose existence has but one purpose: servicing the obscene, destructive extravagance of the wealthiest people ever to walk this earth. Is he right? Are they winning?*

DANIEL MILES: Of course he's right. How could they not be winning? And notice he said that before the banking crisis of 2008. Since then things have got worse.[15] Everywhere

---

[14] < nyti.ms/J9v7oD >

[15] Try this on for size, from 6 March 2012, at *The American Dream* website, '35 Shocking Statistics That Prove That Things Have Gotten Worse In America' < bit.ly/L7r2Ch >

austerity, Athens, Riot Dog,[16] Madrid, Portland, Wall Street, St Pauls, UK riots, food banks, payday loans, Bedroom Tax, benefit sanctions, evictions, disabled suicides. Not worse for the 1% mind you. Oh no. There're getting exactly what they want.

Loukanikos the Riot Dog in action (Athens, May 2011).

And as we type this up, here in the UK, we are heading for more social security cuts, including a social security 'cap' which will throw children born into large families whose parents become ill, disabled, or otherwise fall down the wage ladder, into inevitable poverty. And from that start,

---

[16] We are remembering Loukanikos the Riot Dog, here. Though we see there are other riot dogs who participated on the side of protesters in Athens from 2008 onwards. Two other such dogs were Kanellos and Thodoris, though some claim that Loukanikos and Thodoris are in fact the same dog. Interestingly, these dogs preferred to keep by the protesters rather than the police, which suggests the possibility that even dogs possess a higher moral sense than the 1%. See < bit.ly/KkkqQf > - Loukanikos has several Facebook pages, and he features in a video montage here < on.fb.me/1aq9qId > where we see him 'at ease in his natural riot habitat', this phrase borrowed from a caption to a photograph of Loukanikos here < bit.ly/1aq9KGT >

the statistics show that things are unlikely to get better. Those born into poverty tend to stay there, for a variety of reasons, and they generally suffer worse health and die younger than rich people.[17] They might as well drop toxic gas on the streets where poor people live, specially formulated to ruin the health of all who breathe it in. That looks like war to me. But it's a particularly nasty, obnoxious and immoral war, not least because it harms children.[18] And our right-wing Conservative-led government knows full well the effects their policies will have. The experts tell them; they show them the evidence. People like you and me write letters to them. We post our concerns in our blogs. And as the weeks pass, disputed conjecture about what the future will bring becomes the cold fact of what is happening now, in the present. And it's nasty. Brutal. Inhuman. Psychopathic.

So yes, they're winning, all right. And how they must be loving it. They look on us as nasty paupers who don't work to make profit for them, and now we must pay the price. How we are going to suffer. And how we are going to die! Deprived of food and heating, burdened by illness and depression and the oh-so smug voices of our rulers bellowing from the TV, we will just give up and die. Set up a news

---

[17] See this *Wikipedia* 'Cycle of Poverty' article < bit.ly/1eVP6Bp >, the report from the Joseph Rowntree Foundation *The Costs of Child Poverty for Individuals and Society* < bit.ly/1kFcSsf >, and this from the UK's *Child Poverty Action Group* < bit.ly/1dVtvH1 >

[18] And to the reader who looks askance at us and demands to know how we dared to use the word 'evil' in the title of our book, we will reply *how dare we not.*

alert on the internet, and you'll see the horror of it on your screen every day.

So the question is not really 'are they winning', because of course they are. The question needs to be: What tricks are they using to keep everyone subdued, to keep everyone complicit in the evil they are perpetrating? Why do so many people accept what is happening as if it were simply inevitable? Why do they react to these moral evils as if they were natural evils that no one can do anything about?

Obviously, the people we stand against, those who control the System, those who benefit from it, those in government who serve the 1% - obviously they must have a very powerful capacity to, what shall we say, brainwash people? Or at least manipulate them in effective ways. Part of this method is surely evident in the constant drip-drip-drip of bias and demonisation regarding disabled people and people out of work?

Absolutely. I have a particular revulsion reserved for people who try to sow seeds of hate to further their own selfish ends. Notice how the Conservative government, in bringing in policies that are inevitably going to harm the poorest and most vulnerable people in society, and therefore risk a backlash of opposition and objection, quickly find ways to divide this group of vulnerable people into competing factions that can be baited to rip each other's throats out. They put it to the person in a low-wage job, 'Do you really want your taxes going to provide the social security payments of shirkers and skivers who are too lazy to work, or to pay for the benefits of sick and disabled people who are, on the whole, faking their conditions anyway?'[19]

Of course, such people on low wages should not be taxed in the first place.

Of course not. But the drip-drip-drip of misinformation keeps dribbling from the mouths of our rulers and masters, telling the most vulnerable, those struggling with long hours and dismal pay, that the country is in crisis, that social security claimants in league with the last Labour government have brought this country to its knees, and the only solution is austerity, the fashionable pretext by which suffering can be imposed on the poorest and most vulnerable, the sick and disabled. But no suffering for the richest, of course. Pay rises, bonuses, tax cuts, tax avoidance, tax havens, rocketing property prices, rocketing rents paid by the abject class whom they invite to sign their exploitative rental agreements - that's what they take for themselves. And the deviousness of their evil is to make the ordinary, poor abused low-pay, zero-hours contract worker think that they themselves are the sole author of their degrading plight. This is what the rich tell each other, that to deflect the blame for the suffering you are causing to poor people, make sure the stupid bloody fools are convinced that they are to blame for their own suffering. They must be made to believe that the only reason as to why they are not enjoying the lavish life-

---

[19] See these from the *Guardian* < bit.ly/KmrgVb > < bit.ly/1abB2WQ > and this from *Ekklesia*, the Christian political thinktank < bit.ly/1atGDT5 >

styles of the rich and super-rich, is because they are just too inadequate to simply pick up what is lying right there before them. In a meritocracy where anyone can apply themselves to 'getting on', who is it who is appropriately blamed for anyone's lack of merit, for their lack of social mobility, for failing to get their children out of the squalid class they were born into, and into a class higher up (envisioned via some ludicrous metaphor of climbing a mountain, or climbing a ladder where at the top you don't do anything productive like fix the roof, but live in material luxury, exploiting as many people 'lower down' as you can)? The person you blame for lacking merit is simply the person who lacks merit.

This attitude towards those who lack merit conflates two types of people; on the one hand we have the person whose skills and abilities are limited because this is just the fact about the attributions that fate has dealt them, and on the other hand, the person who is simply lazy or criminal, the person who could 'get on', as you say, but simply can't be bothered. We have a System under which there are powerful incentives to pursue your own advantage and enjoy the fruits of your labour, but this second type of person is just too shiftless to bother, or more interested in pursuing a life of criminality.

Which of course is just stupid, and undermines the very view that generates it: if it is rational to pursue your own interests, it cannot be rational to neglect them by not bothering to profit from your merits, or throw all into permanent jeopardy by taking up the life of a criminal. In other words, the person who does not exercise their merits is in fact the person who never had those merits to begin with. And to the extent that we may think merits can be nurtured and developed, they lack even the talent to investigate the possibility of this option. Yet, in the nasty world of neoliberal capitalism, this person is vilified for their inadequacies, and blamed for the fact that they don't take advantage of the possibility for social mobility that is open to all.

Social mobility is open only to those who have the sorts of merit that are needed for realising it, and whether you have those merits or not is down to pure luck. I have always thought that the notion that social mobility should be regarded as an appropriate remedy for anyone disappointed by poor wages, by poor prospects, by precarity, is a bit like believing that in a game like musical chairs, where twenty people are all vying for the only two chairs that are available, the solution is to add another chair. Yet that is no solution at all. Almost everyone, just as before, is without a chair.

Well, the person who gets to sit on the third chair is happy enough, we may suppose. But the fundamental inequality, *the grossly unfair and abusive quality of the game itself* persists. And this is how the carping on about social mobility works: it blames the victim for their plight. It doesn't say that if you can't find employment that is because there are too few jobs for everybody to have one, it says that you cannot get the job that would otherwise be waiting for you, because you lack the gumption to get qualified, or are too stupid to figure out how to get the training you need, or worse: it is simply your own fault that you do not have those personal qualities, or gift of intelligence, that you need to be accepted onto the course. *So more fool you.* You (they sneer), like everyone else, deserve exactly what you have got, and if that means low wages, no wages, zero-hours contracts, social security payments meted out begrudgingly with sanctions attached like decorative ribbons, *that's just your tough luck, mate.* But the glaring fact in this, the elephant (it's always an elephant) that is stomping around the room, is that a million jobs - could be two, three million, maybe more - are simply not there: people haven't got jobs because *there aren't enough jobs.* It's the sort of thing you could teach a dog.

If it's that obvious, how is it possible for people, some people at any rate, to be complicit in being blamed as victims? Why isn't such a supposedly crass technique of manipulation exposed for the elephant that it is?

When people blame the victim for their misfortune (sexual abuse, rape, exploitation, unemployment, illness) it is because they are trying to justify something that they perceive as inherently unjust. They know it is unjust, and both accuser and onlooker do not, naturally, want to suffer such misfortune themselves. They want power over the misfortune. They want to think they have what is needed to avoid it. And this they must have if victims of misfortunes are the authors of their own suffering, and with respect to such suffering, someone may think, they would never themselves be so inept as to stumble into it. The more the victim is at fault, the safer everyone else is. I would suggest the following

The elephant that no one can see, no longer in the room, roams free, wreaking havoc and mayhem at every turn.

three slightly differing perspectives as to why people might be inclined to think this way.

First, the idea that there is injustice in the world and in society frightens them and upsets their world view (that effort is always rewarded, that healthy eating will keep at bay all illnesses, and so on and so forth), so they try to explain it away as not really existing. Those who suffer misfortune must have done something to deserve it.

Secondly, if the world really is unjust, then they themselves might fall victim to its injustice, so they are motivated to deny that there is in fact any genuine injustice, and from

that point take the smallest step to the conviction that anyone suffering a misfortune has ended up that way through
some blameworthy action, and for that fact deserves what
they get.

Thirdly, they are themselves engaged in some sort of
unjust behaviour and are trying to justify their own wrong-
doing. This category of person includes the rapist who
believes he was provoked by his victim's scanty attire, the
mugger who really believes that someone who ventures
alone into a dark alley really deserves to be beaten and
robbed, and the employer who could pay more than the
minimum wage but does not do so because he believes those
who are inferior to him deserve no better treatment.

*And that takes us back to the notion of social mobility, and the
idea that everyone can control where they end up in society
(educated or not, wielding power or not, wealthy or not, in
control of others or in the control of others). There is merit, I
think (if I may phrase it this way) in looking more closely at
what is happening when people say that social mobility is a
solution to a problem. We should ask two straightforward
questions: (1) What is the problem in response to which social
mobility is presented as the solution? And (2) is it in fact a
solution to this problem?*

The problem that concerns us here is of course the problem
this book addresses, the problem of a System which is
destructive and immoral, that imposes hardships, pain and
suffering on those it exploits (and especially on the children
of those it exploits), with the objective of benefiting those

richest people at the very top, who like parasites, suck up all the work and toil and effort expended by those whom they get to work for them. Though with respect to the question of social mobility, the emphasis that is made by the 1% focuses on inequality. The System is governed by a vicious inequality, and the basic facts of this abhorrence cannot be easily denied. The solution offered focuses not on the System which causes the problem, but on each individual who may (or may not) be complaining about the inequality they suffer. In short, they are told that if you don't like the indignity of exploitation (actually, they don't usually make any reference to this concept), of impoverishing wages, zero-hours contracts, the indignity of unemployment, *then get ahead.* Improve your own personal merit, or better still, find a way to exploit your own workers by starting your own enterprise. Be motivated as we are, by greed, by power, by status. In order not to be treated badly, all you have to do is become a bad person yourself. And if you fail in this endeavour? Well, don't blame us, don't blame the System. Learn to live with the fact that you deserve to be treated like scum.

The ill-thought-out game of musical chairs where twenty people are vying for two chairs is not made more agreeable in any meaningful sense by adding a third chair, as you say.

It isn't the chairs that are the problem, it is the very concept of the idiotic game itself.

Indeed, so of course, social mobility is not really a solution to the problem of an inherently unequal System, it just looks like it is something of a solution, or is the only solution in

town, for people who cannot see (or do not want to see) beyond blaming each individual person for their own unfortu-
nate plight. But we must remind ourselves that the misfortune suffered here is not that of a natural evil, but is a moral
evil, brought about (should we say perfected?) by people
with wishes and schemes and intentions, who seek their
own benefit at the expense of others, who relish the power
they wield, and perhaps also relish the feeling of the presence of that power when they see other people suffering
when it is deployed. Deployed like weapons whose purpose
is not so much destruction, but intimidation, humiliation, of
'teaching lessons' to those demonised as scroungers, of attempting to legitimise a hatred cast over all those who, in
being afflicted by a grossly unequal System, pursue their
entitlements within the social security system.[20] As Warren
Buffett remarked, it is the rich class that is perpetrating a
war on all those it exploits. He thinks the rich have won
already, and maybe he is right, all that is left to its victims as
they lie bleeding and in pain in the shabby ruins of capitalism is to wail our outrage - and some, like you and me, will
even keep jabbing our fingers at the air, pointing towards the
elephant, crying, 'Look! Look!'

*Just before we conclude for today, can you say something
about your observation that social mobility can be seen as a
sham by imagining a world in which everyone magically*

---

[20] See this video for some thoughts on the cruelty of demonising the
victims of the System < bit.ly/1ja7bkd >

acquires all the capacities and qualifications they could wish for?

Yes, of course. As you know, I always like to test arguments and ideas, wherever possible, with thought experiments. As you will remember, it dawned on me to ask, well, if social mobility is such a wonderful thing - if in particular it should be judged as a sound solution to the problems of inequality - what would happen if everyone who wanted to acquire a skill and have that recognised with qualifications, all ready now to adorn whatever CV they would ideally like to have, could simply be given it?

You're thinking about some sort of social mobility fairy, who tours the land at night, reading everyone's inner thoughts, and waving her magic wand to make real whatever they are thinking?

Exactly. But these are real skills, real abilities. But you can have them just for the wishing. There are no classes to attend, no fees to find, no exams to pass. And what you have is as good as having years of experience.

The social mobility fairy simply re-weaves the fabric of the universe to make it all so ... you wake up and find that you are a qualified plumber or accountant or civil engineer, dentist, veterinarian, IT manager, architect, teacher...

Yes, anything you like. And the upshot? When all the unemployed people go to the Jobcentre the morning after? *There would be no change at all.* All these skilled people are still unemployed, just as they were before. They are still in competition with their peers, just as they were before. One thousand applicants still apply for each job. In fact the social mobility fairy has made the situation worse, because in proportion to the people seeking jobs that are appropriate for people with skills, a far greater number of people are now in competition for the same tiny number of jobs.

If you want to get a job that is commensurate with your skills, it would be better to wish that the social mobility fairy could take away some of the skills you already have...

Let's conclude with our gaze firmly fixed on that Jobcentre. Here is another elephant that not everyone can see: *unemployment.* This is one of Warren Buffett's most powerful weapons in the armoury that he and his kind target on those they exploit. Unemployment is essential for the System to function. *They would not want to fix it, even if they could.* The worst possible thing would be for unemployment to fall to levels low enough for workers to be able to dictate to their employers the rates of pay that are meted out to them. The scarcer the jobs, the easier it is to get away with low wages. And the lower the wages, the greater the exploitation and the gaping gulf between rich and poor grows ever more obscene.

So here is another deceit perpetrated on a gullible electorate: the government of the day, working in the interests of the System, must give the impression that it believes unemployment to be a bad thing, something undesirable that must be tackled and reduced. *Whilst all along it believes no such thing.* It must pretend to jump up and down in joy when the figures show that unemployment is falling, and indeed, apparent proof that policies are reducing unemployment cannot be wholly unwelcome. The confidence trick must be maintained, after all. But their intention is not really to lower the levels of unemployment - that would be a disaster for capitalism - but merely to present the illusion, no different from a magician on stage, that they both care about the plight of the unemployed and have policies to deal with it. But that is a complete sham. The reality is that they need at least a certain level of unemployment sufficient to terrorise the 99% by demonising those the System chooses not to employ in order to make those who do have a job thankful for their minimum wage or zero-hours contract, or otherwise grateful that they are being exploited.

But they don't see themselves as people exploited...

Indeed they do not. They think they are pursuing their own self-interest, when in reality they are working for the self-interest of the 1%. This is perhaps the least important part of the problem - that the 99% are being deceived in this way. The real problem stems from the sheer levels of pain and suffering that the System causes in order to maintain its ascendancy.

Welfare cuts
KEEP
CALM
AND
CARRY
ON
KILLING
THE DISABLED
Over 10,600 dead due to Tory welfare reforms
No Future
under the Conservatives

6

Austerity – the Biggest Con Ever

KARL GRUBER: *The gap between rich and poor has grown faster in Britain than in any other developed country over recent decades.*[21] *Taxes for the rich have been cut, whilst social security benefits for the poor are being scaled back. Public services, including the National Health Service, and virtually all services provided by local authorities are being cut. All in the name of austerity.*

DANIEL MILES: All with the ludicrously false claim that our country is too poor to provide these services at former levels, that we simply do not have the money, and that we must cut public expenditure or face some dire calamity that will bring ruin to us all.

These claims are not just false. They are intended to deceive us, to bully us into accepting the need for so-called austerity.

The need for austerity is a myth. A total lie, designed to make the richest 1% richer still, and to keep the rest of us, the 99%,

---

[21] This is from the *Telegraph* website < bit.ly/1jFDvcX >

in our place, ready to serve our masters as slaves in all but name. I believe that you have been researching the facts.

And the facts are deeply disturbing, not because there really is a problem eating away at the state's finances, but precisely because there is not a problem. The present 'crisis' is entirely made up, a complete fiction. Here's what I have found out. Anyone can check these facts. We will put our sources in the footnotes.

At the beginning of the twentieth century, the National Debt stood at about 30 percent of GDP. It rose above 150 percent in World War I and stayed relatively high until dropping below 100 percent in the early 1960s. By the 1970s, debt declined to 50 percent of GDP, and dropped to 25 percent by 1990. The National Debt began to increase again in the aftermath of the worldwide financial crisis of 2008, and today is the same as it was in the late 1960s.[22]

But this does not mean that there is a 'debt crisis'. It means that the UK government owes £1.19 trillion - which is approximately 75% of the total UK economy for one year.[23]

In fact, the only time since the early 1700s when the national debt has been lower than it is now was during the period between the latter decades of the 19th century and the start of World War I. The level of debt we have now is completely normal. It is a feature of the economic system. It is nothing more than an aspect of how it works.

---

[22] The detailed chart from the *UK Public Spending* website from which we derive this paragraph is here < bit.ly/1fwaUS2 >

[23] See these figures at the BBC, for mid-2013 < bbc.in/1jMVnm9 >

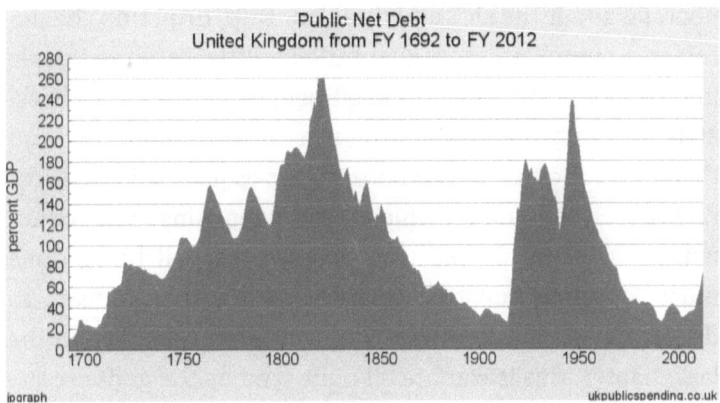

Source: UK Public Spending < bit.ly/1dJ22ZF >

So our government is simply lying to us? That today's debt constitutes a problem is a complete and utter fiction, concocted and spread by the richest 1% and their friends in government so as to keep the rest of us under their heel, and to 'justify' the government's 'difficult' decisions to slam the most vulnerable, the sick, the disabled, the unemployed, with cuts to their entitlements within the Welfare State.

This is what the figures tell us. We must speak directly to the person who is reading this: *the government is lying to you.* It is lying to all of us. It distorts facts and figures to suit its purpose. And it's purpose? To make themselves and their millionaire friends richer, as you say, and to do that by making the rest of us poorer.[24] And its method is to demonise the

---

[24] For more on the need for austerity being a myth, see these
< bit.ly/1fx7LS3 > < bit.ly/1lq4VGP > < bit.ly/1i0H0tK >
< huff.to/1iIPUhO > < bit.ly/1fx8R6e > < bit.ly/Pkazx8 >

poor, lie about the sick and disabled. Drip, drip, drip the deceit to a compliant press that little by little deceives people into thinking that most disabled people are frauds, deliberately merging the disabled person with the criminal. And that's why the title of our book stands as justified and accurate. The System under which this is happening is an abomination. And the people who oversee the evil being done must be, surely must be regarded as less than human, as deeply flawed in some way. Yes, as Buffett remarked in the last chapter, this is warfare all right. And by the gods are the weakest among us suffering.[25] Those in power have set themselves a clear and simple agenda, and that is to provide tax cuts (and all other manner of advantages) to the rich, whilst dishing out the evil filth of poverty and fear to sick and disabled people, and more generally demonising and heaping abuse on pretty much all social security claimants. It seems clear to some of us that the Conservative government is on course to dismantle the Welfare State.

There appears to be some sort of irrational obsession at work here, something which were it to be encountered in an individual would conclude with some sort of mental health diagnosis.

---

[25] There is evidence that under new draconian social security rules, vulnerable people are being driven to suicide. Some researchers think the numbers are in the thousands. In other contexts, this would be designated genocide. See this at the *Express* website
< dexpr.es/1bKc5m8 > See also this at the *Guardian* website
< bit.ly/NOcdWq > and this at the *Independent* website
< ind.pn/18zIx3v >

It seems impossible to believe that apparently normal people, who have families and friends, who in all the usual ways are regarded as responsible people - I am thinking of David Cameron the Prime Minister, and the millionaire members of his cabinet - should set out purposefully to bring destitution

to so many people. It is as if they have some sort of burning revenge eating at their brains, which will not let them rest until its objectives have been satisfied. It's as if their own position of power must be continually verified by using it to hurt people. The bully, of course, is the person who relishes bringing harm to others, for the sheer thrill of witnessing other people in distress.[26]

---

[26] Jon Ronson muses in his *The Psychopath Test* (2011, 34) that 'It really could be that many of our political and business leaders suffer from

There is something deeply disturbing going on in UK politics at the moment ... well, and in other places, as well, obviously. But the driving force behind the surge of moral evil that is affecting so many innocent people is the bizarrely simple agenda set by the 1% at the top: they want more, and they don't care if in getting more they hurt people and wreck the planet.

It seems odd that many people are simply unaware of the immorality and the absurdity of what is happening. We see in this article that, as of October 2012, Chancellor George Osborne has already cut social security spending by £18 billion, with a further £10 billion to follow.[27] Yet at the very same time, multinational corporations and the richest billionaires and millionaires are managing to avoid their liabilities to pay UK tax to the tune of £70 billion a year.[28] Even if these figures turn out not to be as accurate as we may prefer them, it

---

Antisocial or Narcissistic Personality Disorder and they do the harmful, exploitative things they do because of some mad striving for unlimited success and excessive admiration. *Their mental disorders might be what rules our lives'* (italics ours). And this page at the *Signs of the Times* website provides a short overview, with a number of links, outlining the distressing reality, that in all reality, 'psychopaths rule our world' < bit.ly/1gq37pZ > So consider the probability that when a politician is wringing their hands, facing the agony of 'making tough decisions', they in fact feel nothing whatever for the people they are about to hammer, intending only to fool you with their sham concern. Such a person, lacking what is required to be fully human, should not be put in charge of anything more sentient than a pile of rocks.

[27] This is at *Money* website, October 2012 < bit.ly/Ne7xJw >

[28] Article at the *New Statesmen* website, November 2011 < bit.ly/1lq9HE4 >

is stunningly obvious that far from needing to cut the social security budget, he could in fact significantly increase it (even double it), and still have change left over to the value of billions of pounds, if only he decided to lift a finger and make sure the richest in our society actually paid the amount of tax they are supposed to pay.

But instead, it is the poorest and most vulnerable people who are hounded by Work Capability Assessments, by the Bedroom Tax, by sanctions, and who are demeaned by the indignity of having to queue at food banks because they cannot afford to feed themselves or their children.[29]

And this is nothing short of truly despicable. It shames all of us for allowing it to happen. It is the manifestation of wilful evil that is being threaded through the tapestry of our present-day society. It makes life in modern Britain nasty and sickening. It makes our politicians criminals, liable under Human Rights legislation. Will they face justice? Of course not.

---

[29] See this at the *Trussell Trust* website < bit.ly/1c1xhSf >

7

Skivers, Scroungers and Parasites

KARL GRUBER: *We have mentioned a number of times[30] how the Conservative-led government and other agents and supporters of the 1%, including naturally enough the right-wing press,[31] have set about demonising social security recipients of all hues (unemployed, sick and disabled, single parents, and so forth). For instance, at the Turn2us website, we find that in consequence, the public now vastly overestimates the numbers of people who commit benefit fraud, with significant numbers believing that most claims are fraudulent, whilst many now see claimants as less deserving than they did 20 years ago.[32] Others, rightly, defend the entitlements of claimants who are stigmatised by peddlers of hate, and this is of course work that*

---

[30] See above, pages 52, 60, 63, 67-8.

[31] Here at the *False Economy* website are four examples from early 2011 of false and misleading headlines in the *Daily Express* which aim to demonise social security benefits claimants, < bit.ly/1iv7OFS > and here are the lies and distortions of those headlines exposed < bit.ly/1flLzPA >

[32] See this page at the *Turn2us* website < bit.ly/1ite4d5 > See their reports from November 2012, *Read Between the Lines: confronting the myths about the benefits system* < bit.ly/PlSleJ > and *Benefits Stigma in Britain* < bit.ly/1gfUZMm >

we wholeheartedly support. May I suggest however that today
we examine this question from the opposite perspective, and
take a look at how the capitalist System works, to find out who
the real parasites are.

DANIEL MILES: Yes, of course. But first I want to make this
important, if brief, remark. We now have clear evidence of
the outrageous immorality of government policy in its drive
to protect the richest in society at the expense of the poorest
and the most vulnerable, not just in the sense that the poor
will be a bit poorer than they were before, but in the sense
that the poor will be made to suffer, to cringe at the nastiness of modern living as the Conservative government is
shaping it. And the government is doing this with wilful
intent, purposefully finding ways to make the poorest and
most vulnerable suffer.

Instead of making the tax system more fair, and taxing
the richest people a little more - a mere slither of a little
extra considered as a proportion of their massive wealth -
the government has reduced the rate of income tax for the
richest[33] and will cut deeply into the incomes and services

---

[33] We have mentioned the tax cut for the rich (to be implemented from
April 2013), above, on pages 53 and 68.

Here is an interesting observation: 'The number of millionaires who
will benefit from David Cameron's April tax cut has soared to 13,000.
Experts had predicted that 8,000 people earning £1million a year would
get an average tax cut of almost £100,000 - thanks to the PM and
Chancellor George Osborne's decision to cut the 50p top rate of tax to
45p. But new figures reveal the number of people earning at least £1m a
year has rocketed to 13,000, despite the economy being on the brink of a

needed desperately by the sick and disabled, the elderly, and other vulnerable groups.

And the cuts are going to slice deep. The government wants to 'save' £75.2 billion, and the areas being cut the most are social care and welfare.

In other words, the most vulnerable in society are being hunted down to pay the price for the failure of the capitalist System, for the incompetence of government, and the incompetence of the banks. And all to satisfy the greed of the richest.

Dr Simon Duffy in his report *A Fair Society? How the Cuts Target Disabled People*,[34] finds that:

Using the government's own figures, it is clear that by 2015 ... benefits for disabled people and the poorest will ... have been cut by £18 billion, a cut of about 20%.

When we look at the combined impact of all the cuts we find:

- People in poverty (21% of the population) bear 39% of all cuts.

---

triple-dip recession. The income of Brits who earned more than £1m last year was an astonishing £27.4billion' *Mirror News* website, 3 February 2013 < bit.ly/N2pCcP > Note this from the *Mail Online* website, 23 May 2010: 'Of the 29 Ministers entitled to attend Cabinet meetings, 23 have assets and investments estimated to be worth more than £1million' < dailym.ai/1ivrWrB >

[34] Published on behalf of the *Campaign for a Fair Society*, available here < bit.ly/ND37fc > at the *Campaign for Welfare Reform* website < bit.ly/1emvAg3 >

- Disabled people (8% of the population) bear 29% of all cuts.
- People with severest disabilities (2% of the whole population) bear 15% of all cuts.

Not only are the cuts in general being targeted at people in poverty, but there is a specific emphasis on targeting disabled people. You cannot argue against that sort of inhuman discrimination, because the person you are trying to argue with is plainly not open to, or not interested in rational argument.

The only explanation for this that makes any sense is to understand that Cameron, Osborne and the rest, literally have something wrong with them. They are incapable of the normal sort of moral thinking that guides the daily lives of you and me. They display the psychology that we see in psychopaths, that is, people who literally do not have feelings for other people, but use them like insensible objects, as resources for their own self-serving schemes.[35]

And that idea, that those with power over others may use them as a resource to exploit, is a fair characterisation of the capitalist System, is it not? It is the core theme we aim to develop in this book.

Exploitation is the complete and defining characteristic of the System to which we are opposed - to which any reasonable person with the slightest capacity for moral sentiment

---

[35] See Stout 2005.

must be opposed... There are two distinct dimensions to this immoral exploitation. On the one hand we have *human exploitation*, which we explained briefly earlier on with our example of the umbrella factory [in Chapter 2], and *environmental exploitation*, in which those who are deemed to 'own' a natural resource are permitted to exploit it to any degree they wish, irrespective of any wider damage caused, no matter for how long that damage will affect people and the wider environment into the future;[36] not to mention those cases where damage means permanent destruction, loss of habitat and extinction of species, from which no recovery can ever be possible.

And this exploitation is the consequence of the basic tenet, presumption or conviction - held with a sort of maniacal, religious fervour, putting this principle beyond all questioning,

---

[36] There are of course many books, articles and websites which deal with the question as to how the drive for capitalist profit is damaging the environment. The choice of what to examine on this issue is so vast, there seems little point in making our own suggestions, but we urge readers to undertake their own investigation into how dire the situation is becoming. We will, presumably, face the charge that in our sentiments we are ignoring the presence of environmental laws and measures to provide at least a basic standard of protection and preservation, at least in some countries and locations. Our view is that such legislation, even in places where it is scrupulously applied, is for all intents and purposes inadequate to the point of useless. Any success suggested for one location will be undone by devastation occurring elsewhere. When the final tally is made by historians in future generations, it will look as if we made no effort at all in the interest of protecting and preserving the environment.

*making it a sort of doctrinal creed any challenge to which
would be a sort of outrageous sacrilege - that the sole objective
of companies and corporations is to make profit for their
shareholders.*

It's that simple. This little idea, this little unquestioned
assumption supported and promoted by those who benefit
from its application, has brought down upon us for generation after generation, in this country and right across the
globe, such untold misery and suffering, and even now, at
the beginning of a new, technologically advanced century,
threatens yet more torment and wretchedness for the fore-
seeable future.

*But the idea that companies and corporations exist solely for
the purpose of making profit for their shareholders seems to
derive from an even more basic principle - that the interests of
those with property are, if not always, at least generally
regarded as having a greater validity and are worthy of more
urgent attention than the interests of those without property.
Those with property have a higher social standing than those
who lack property. The interests of the first group are worthy
of protecting and advancing; the interests of the second group,
if they merit consideration at all, are essentially unimportant,
and if remedies for this group are ever deemed appropriate,
resources provided for such remedies will be considered a
drain on the property of the first group. And before we know it,
the first group of property owners will be defined as 'deserving
strivers', and the second group will be designated 'undeserving
skivers'.*

Well, there is a devious sort of subtlety at work here that we should expose. The second group of undeserving non-owners of property can acquire the status of deserving strivers by turning up for work and creating the wealth that the owners simply appropriate for themselves. A good slave, surely, can be both appreciated and also rewarded with a few crumbs, even if those crumbs fall short of providing a subsistence living that must be supplemented by tax credits and housing benefit, or other social security benefits. Striving for the wealth of the 1% is commendable, whereas being sick and disabled or unemployed, and claiming one's entitlement within a civilised social security system is not commendable – in fact it is so despicable and so demeaning to the strivers who provide the 1% with their wealth, that claimants will be disproportionately targeted under the guise of austerity [as we saw in the previous chapter]. Even people who themselves are poor, in that condition not because they are not working, but are working under the burden of exploitation, can be persuaded to hate and detest, to some degree, those less fortunate than themselves. Some, it seems, although abused and exploited by the 1% will nevertheless side with their exploiters in developing some degree of detestation for the unemployed, the sick and disabled.

This is a picture of fools being led by bullies.

It is depressing to see it this way. But what we do see is evil, brutish, and a corruption of human rationality, sympathy and compassion. It is the manifestation of power that seeks its own advantage no matter what the cost to those it exploits and abuses.

The unquestioned tenet that corporations and companies exist with the sole purpose of maximising returns to their shareholders creates the imperative to do evil: for it makes legitimate and necessary, once that original tenet is taken up and given its unquestioned status, the exploitation of those without property, who lack any means of sustenance apart from selling their labour. It makes the ongoing evil normal and desirable. And the extent to which any of its perpetrators get anywhere close to acknowledging the moral nastiness of the System that uses people as a resource to exploit is the extent to which the most 'moral' among them will call for another chair to be added to the stupid game of musical chairs [page 55]. And having added the chair, they can shout down to those they exploit, 'Don't like how I am treating you, eh? Well, there's another chair. If you are too weak to wrest it from others who might want to enjoy it, why blame me? All you need to do is work a bit harder and beat others to the marvellous prize of the extra chair.' The extra chair is a con. It solves nothing. It is a chair of distraction. It tricks your eye away from what is really wrong; it opens the door to blaming the victim for their own plight.

But valuing shareholders above everyone else produces the dubious consequence that the measure of how well society is doing is not determined by how well society is doing, but by how well a very tiny elite of wealthy shareholders is doing.

Indeed. So now we have the preposterous claim that because the gross domestic product of the UK is creeping up slightly, then all is fine, or at least going better - when the fact of the matter is that for the vast majority of people, the value of their wage or social security benefit is actually going down, whilst the cost of living is going up.[37] And they call that success!

Another way to look at this is to ask why shareholders should be elevated to this privileged position. Why not throw out maximising returns to shareholders as the objective of corporate activity, and substitute in its place the maximising of employee welfare? The choice to favour shareholders over employees is just another manifestation of the evil we hope to expose in these conversations, the evil of a minority of privileged people living off the labour of those they exploit.

Well, the counterargument will run something like this. Since the shareholder's investment in the company was what made it possible (collectively, anyway) for the company to start up in business, employ people, and sell its products for profit, surely the shareholders deserve the greatest possible return on their investment that the company can get for them?

---

[37] As far as we can see, this general claim about economies doing well whilst ordinary people are doing worse is common across all the western economies. It is generally reflected in the persisting programme of making the rich richer and the poor poorer. The gulf between rich and poor seems set to get wider and wider, the 'better' the economy does.

And on the face of it, there is some plausibility to this view. The one big problem is that almost all shareholders did not purchase initial share offerings, so did not in any way contribute to the start-up costs of the company. They did not in fact contribute anything productive needed for the production of what the company produces.

They simply bought the shares from those who bought the shares from those who bought the shares from those who bought the shares (you get the idea) from those who actually invested in the company when they purchased shares in the initial offering.

Which makes them gamblers. They are gambling both that their shares will pay out handsome annual dividends and that, should they wish to sell their shares, their shares will at that point net them a handsome profit over what they originally paid for them.

But let us ask this question: what have they really purchased when they bought those shares? *I contend that they have purchased someone else's labour.* They have purchased an entitlement under which someone will go to work, providing the company with the manpower it needs to create and sell its products at a profit, and instead of rewarding the worker who made that profit with a higher wage, the quantity of money represented by the 'profit' is paid to someone who, with regard to this enterprise at least, is totally and utterly bone idle.

Here, I contend, is the scrounger, the skiver, the shirker

in the System - here is the person who lives off the work of others whilst contributing nothing themselves whatsoever to generating the dosh that their 'entitlement' provides for them. Here is the parasite who, whilst they suck up the value of other people's efforts, has the barefaced effrontery to shout 'skiver' at others.

And the vile irony here is that the poor unemployed person, who in pursuing their entitlement to social security benefits suffers the indignity of being branded a 'skiver', really does want to work in this exploitative System! It's just that the System cannot provide jobs for everyone who would like to be exploited.

And if you can't work, you will be insulted and vilified as a scrounger, whilst all along the real parasite is no doubt living a few streets away in relative luxury, living a life funded by the efforts of others, at the same time glorying in their status as a worthy person, as a shareholder, the person whom the System is set up to support; and who in these present, horrid, horrid, days is growing richer and richer, while the people who do the actual work which creates that profit grow ever more poor. That society can tolerate some of its members being treated like this is deeply disturbing.

And after the UK riots of August 2011, Prime Minister David Cameron had the audacity to label the rioters' actions as 'criminality, pure and simple'.[38] Well, to be sure, some criminality was present, let us have some confidence in that. But in addition to that was a seething contempt for the System that is hurting so many people, that praises the share-

---

[38] See this at the *Guardian* website < bit.ly/1idzoV5 >

holding parasite, and vilifies the social security claimant -
the System which applauds those with wealth and power for
pursuing what is in their best interests, while condemning
the downtrodden and abused for trying to adopt the same
mentality.

The evil we mean to point out is manifest right here in
this distinction, between those who must work for the benefit of other people, and those others whose privilege sets
them apart as deserving more than the 'skivers' who in actual fact comprise that part of the population from which the
privileged extract their workforce, their slaves in all but
name, who must labour for the benefit of those who exploit
them.

I hope to God that people will one day look back on our
time in astonishment, with a full understanding of how barbaric it was. But the fact that the barbarism is present for us
now, that it is daily in the process of hurting people, that it is
threatening the environment of the planet in deep and disturbing ways, puts upon us a special responsibility to hold it
to account and to find a way to bring it to an end.

*I think you feel as I do, that seeing how our species is behaving,
coming to realise what distorted values fuel the enterprises of
the bullies amongst us, makes us ashamed to be human, and
makes us view the horror of our times with a contempt we can
barely contain.*

And that revulsion must be *our* fuel, and it must be used to
make us *think* and *communicate*, and *find reasons* for saying
why this evil must end. If the aliens we imaged earlier [in

Chapter 4] came and talked to us, we would have to declare that of course we can see our shame, but we understand it, and why we must struggle to be rid of it. We do see the truth of this. We see someone who has purchased an entitlement to be supported on the back of other people's labour.

Let us imagine the umbrella factory we visited in our imaginations [in Chapter 2], but now on a much grander scale, employing thousands of workers, making millions of umbrellas, founded many years ago by an initial share offering that was one of the largest of that decade. And imagine that we look down on one of the workers, who has worked here all his life, now approaching retirement. Like all the other workers he is of course exploited, because the wage he is paid represents only a fraction (perhaps it is half) of the value that is realised by the sale of the umbrellas that he makes. The surplus profit, generated by his efforts, goes to the shareholders.

And let us imagine one of these shareholders. This person did in fact buy their shares in the initial offering, and has been paid dividends on them for many years. And we will explain why, nevertheless, we call this person a parasite, someone who does nothing productive (not with respect to making umbrellas, anyway), but enjoys their material status (maybe the whole of it) on the backs of the efforts of others. Here is the scrounger that the Conservatives will hide away, whilst making every effort to demonise the workers from the factory (let us imagine) who were made redundant after the 2008 financial collapse when the company was restructured, and who now cannot find new jobs.

Let us imagine that the shareholder paid £100,000 for

their shares. A fine some of money, required by the umbrella company, together with all the other sums from all the other shareholders, to buy the factory, all the equipment, delivery vehicles, and whatever else was needed to get the enterprise up and running. And that shareholder is entitled to their dividends for all of eternity. Indeed, this entitlement will pass to their heir, or to whomever they sell their shares to, and after that to whomever *their* heir may be.

And the worker who has worked there all his life? Has he not contributed considerably more? He has made the umbrellas, for a start. But let us imagine that he is exploited to the sum of £10,000 every year;[39] that is, the quantity of umbrellas that he makes over and above the quantity required to cover his wages has a value to the company of £10,000. In ten years, he will have contributed £100,000 worth of free labour to the company, and in the decade after that, the same sum again, and in the decade after that another £100,000, and so, until he retires. Through this exploitative arrangement, he has contributed to the company a sum that is significantly larger than the sum paid by the shareholder, who purchased his shares in the initial offering.

But where is this worker's entitlement? Clearly, he has contributed considerably more than the shareholder. And the shareholder's heir will just keep on getting the handouts. And the worker's heir? Well, they won't get a penny.

The entitlement the shareholder has to the value of the labour that the worker keeps on expending, decade after

---

[39] It's almost certainly going to be more than this, but let's keep the arithmetic simple in order to make our point as clearly as we can.

decade, came from one simple source. Their own pocket, which was deep enough to pay for that entitlement, deep enough to pay for the worker's surplus labour for the whole of his working life, and after that for the labour of the worker who will take his place, and all subsequent workers, for the rest of time.

How different is this to having an entitlement to the value of a slave's labour, in virtue of the fact that the exploiter 'owns' their slave? There is no difference at all. The only difference, we will try to explain to the incredulous aliens, is to be found in the words we use: the exploiter does not 'own' the person who works for their advantage, no, it's more subtle than that - *they own shares in the company he works for!*

But it comes to the same thing. And therein lies our shame, and our plea to the aliens that we are not all immoral monsters, manipulating our social relationships so that some (the wealthy, with property) may live in material comfort whilst others (the poor, those lacking property) slave - yes, literally slave - to provide for them.

This arrangement is nasty. We detest it because it deserves to be detested. It makes our species nasty for tolerating it, and it makes our species stupid, so utterly stupid, for allowing its realisation to destroy our planet, bit by bit, habitat by habitat, making it inevitable that in all probability, perhaps in the next few centuries, the one species we can be sure will go extinct is homo sapiens itself.

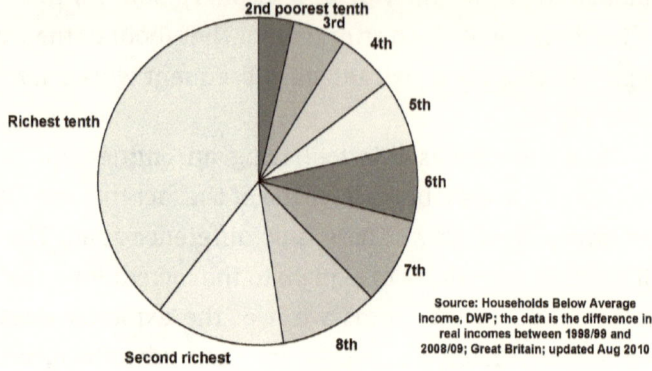

Figure 2

Four-fifths of the total increase in incomes over the last decade has gone to those with above-average incomes and two-fifths has gone to those in the richest tenth

Source: Households Below Average Income, DWP; the data is the difference in real incomes between 1998/99 and 2008/09; Great Britain; updated Aug 2010

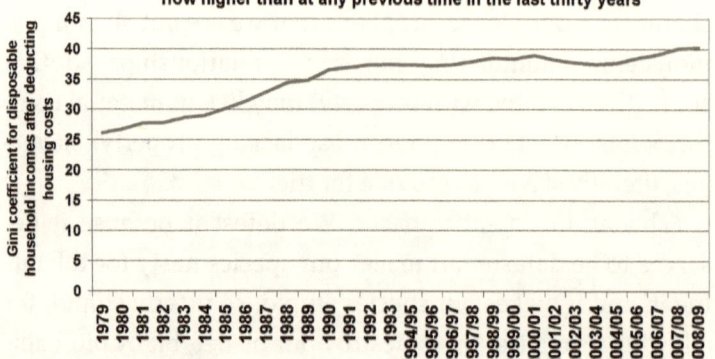

Figure 3

The gini coefficient measure of overall income inequality in the UK is now higher than at any previous time in the last thirty years

Source: Households Below Average Income, DWP (1994/95 onwards) and the Family Expenditure Survey (earlier years) obtained via data published by the IFS; UK; updated Aug 2010

The Gini coefficient shown in Figure 3, measuring overall income inequality, is now higher than at any previous time in the last 30 years. A value of 0 would show that all households had the same income, and a value of 100 would show that a single household had all the country's income.

8

Paradise Denied

KARL GRUBER: *We live in a society whose purpose is the creation, maintenance, and expansion of massive inequalities.*[40] *Everything that happens is geared to this singular objective.*

DANIEL MILES: Tony Benn captures the essence of this appallingly evil situation with what on the face of it appears to be a rather innocuous phrase: 'The pleasures of some are bought at the expense of others.'[41] We say this is evil because, when sketched in the broadest brushstrokes, on the global scale, what is at stake is the survival of civilisation itself, because if the environment is degraded beyond a certain limit, the activities that sustain our civilisation will cease, and the civilisation itself will cease. What level of degradation can be inflicted before significant problems arise can be debated. But the link between bad practice and the

---

[40] See the diagrams opposite. We do not actually discuss the details of the pie chart and the graph we found at poverty.org.uk, but we think they speak for themselves. They show the facts of the inequalities that so disturb us.
[41] Benn, Letter 38 (2009, 149).

failure of civilisation is certain. In this assessment lie the endeavours of environmentalists, who, it seems, cannot be said to be winning anything other than minor battles, and the fight for a safer, more sustained future seems to be going very badly. The major issue of our time is of course global warming and, year on year, the quantities of carbon dioxide being emitted into the atmosphere keep rising, without the slightest glimmer of that output stabilising, let alone actually reducing. As things stand, global temperatures by the end of the twenty-first century will be dangerously higher than they are now, and the impact on human populations and our quality of life will be devastating. This ridiculous, mad, irresponsible drive for destruction has one main impetus: the exploitation of the many by the few who benefit from all the things that are done, all the making and doing, moving, crafting and shaping, all the thinking and creating - all the things that everyone does, observed by the aliens we imagined earlier [Chapter 4, page 42], done under the direction and control of the 1% of the population to keep their Profit Machine working, making their lives as materially comfortable as possible, whilst reducing the lives of those who actually produce the goods that the Profit Machine spews out to the lowest level that they can get away with. As Figure 2 shows, the increase in incomes in recent years has flowed disproportionately into the pockets of the rich which, if bloated before, are fairly bursting with the value of other people's labour now.

This is evil, not just because it is unjust (any fool can see it is unjust), nor because its cumulative affects edge us closer and closer to environmental catastrophe (any fool can see

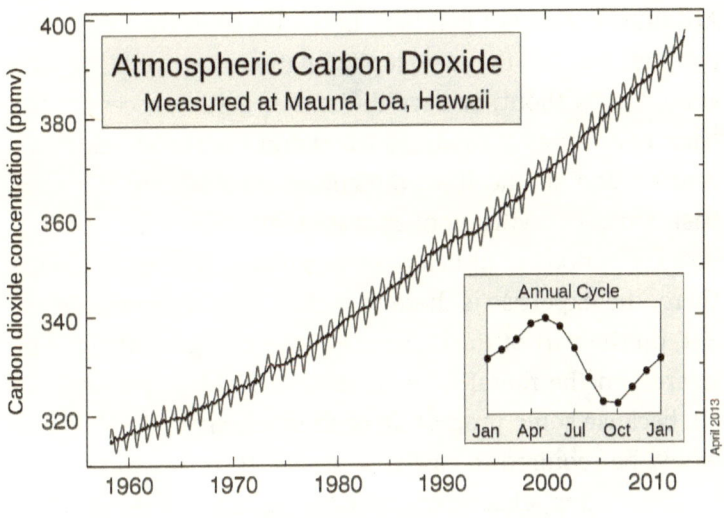

Figure 4

Carbon Dioxide Concentrations

This figure shows the history of atmospheric carbon dioxide concentrations as directly measured at Mauna Loa, Hawaii. This curve is known as the Keeling curve, and is an essential piece of evidence of the man-made increases in greenhouse gases that are believed to be the cause of global warming.

that that is so), but also because it hurts people right here, right now. It is a System invented, implemented and controlled by bullies, and it is a detestable thing.

Here is something that perhaps we could not say until fairly recently, perhaps not until after the Second World War: given our ongoing level of expertise, certainly in the most basic and essential things, in construction, food production, medicine, sanitation, manufacturing technology - our society should be a paradise for all.

Absolutely. And not just here in the UK or in the developed nations, but in the developing nations as well. No one should go without, or have difficulties getting access to the basic necessities of food and water and shelter and clothing. And no one should have difficulties in obtaining the most basic fruits of civilisation: education, medical care, and support for periods of ill-health or in old age. The resources are there, the expertise is there to make use of those resources. Yet, on the part of the richest few, the 1% again, there is no interest in the moral imperative to create this paradise for all, because some proportion of their massive pile of wealth would be required to easily, so easily, turn this world from the frustrating, chaotic mess that it is, into that paradise for all - no hunger, no disease, no sorrow or lamentation that can be mended by merely the application of know-how, expertise, and the building of the infrastructure needed to bring it all about. A little effort, and all would be well, for everyone, everywhere. There is nothing difficult in this. Except for the damned Profit Machine blocking our way: except for the bullies who rule our world and maintain its misery for the satisfaction of their own comfort.

Here lies the explanation, I think, of why the Occupy protesters refused to make a straight answer to the simple question, *What do you want?* The question itself already defines the context in which the answer must be placed. It requires that the answer make sense within the context of the ongoing enterprise of the Profit Machine and the value System of the rich. Answers which cannot show how the Profit Machine can continue essentially unimpeded would be ruled inadmissible and laughed away. In other words, there is no possible answer to the question *What do you want?* because the parameters of the answer have already been decided. *What do you want so long as the capitalist System remains essentially unchanged, and the many are compelled to work for the benefit of the few?* makes no sense, because the dominance of the few over the many *is the problem*.

What we want is a new System altogether. What we want is a revolution, a complete turning around of what we have, to make a completely different arrangement. A System which doesn't create problems and destroy all hope of a paradise for all, but actually solves the problems that are at the moment blocking our path to a paradise for all.

I think we should be clear about what we mean by this notion of 'paradise for all'. Precision is not really helpful, here, and I think our task can be accomplished by applying the broad brushstrokes I mentioned earlier. The 'paradise' we think everyone is entitled to, or the 'good life', as some people call it, can be thought of in this simple but very powerful way - paradise is realised to the extent that people progress to the higher levels in Maslow's Hierarchy of Needs [see page 32]. There is no paradise, no good life, for people lacking even the most basic needs. Indeed, the most basic needs are required for even staying alive. That is why anyone's suffering the deprivation of clean water, for example, is suffering an evil. It is in itself an evil, and it is evil again for the fact that there will be people whose effort, whose easy effort, can in a moment relieve that misery. And so on up the scale. If a country's rulers cannot provide security, then that is an evil, and if they need help from outside to do it, and that help is not forthcoming from those who can easily provide it, then that is another evil. If people who organise the daily routine of workers do not accommodate the realities of family life, of caring for children and supporting the communities which maintain and sustain family life, then here again is evil, the wilful decision to diminish the human spirit for love and cherishing and being together instead of providing for it and enhancing it to the maximum degree possible. And, if provision is in place for the more basic needs, but provision for education is lacking, then here is yet another evil, for the satisfaction of the common human capacity for curiosity and for learning how to do things is essential for living well and flourishing. That it could be provided for, yet is not, is no less evil than all the other deplorable things listed here.

And the present capitalist System which so completely dominates all our lives is a stinking, foul and contemptible fount of such evil. It inhibits human flourishing. It makes miserable what should be delightful. It brings distress to people who deserve comfort and support. It makes a commodity of everything, yet values nothing that is truly good. The bottom line is what counts, and the poor, stupid human beings who slave for it can cry into the storm for sustenance, because, to be sure, if it doesn't benefit the 1%, it ain't going to happen.

Maslow's Hierarchy of Needs as a Metaphorical Mountain

Given the gross inequalities between the powerful, controlling, owning, 1% of the population (represented by the figure near to the top of the mountain) and the exploited, toiling, abused 99% of the population (represented by the figure near the bottom), it seems obvious that those amongst the 1% who succeed best in satisfying their needs on Maslow's schema are able to do so *as a direct result of exploiting the 99%*. Those of us at the bottom have difficulty in flourishing as well as we might precisely because the 1% bend us to their will in making us work for the Profit Machine. The priority of the 1% is to maximise their own flourishing; their priority for the 99% is that we should serve the very same end. Again, we are merely a resource whose exploitation serves the primary purpose of benefiting the rich. Thus is our existence tolerated by the 1%.

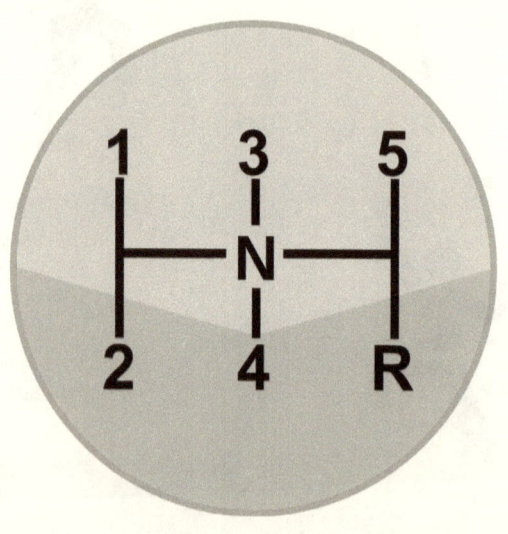

9

The Stupidity of Work

KARL GRUBER: *At a symposium organised by* New York Magazine, *and published as 'New York Environmental Teach-In'*
by Elizabeth Barlow in the March 1970 issue,[42] *American archi-*
tect, systems theorist, author, designer, inventor, and futurist
R. Buckminister Fuller (1895-1983) remarked:

We must do away with the absolutely specious notion that
everybody has to earn a living. It is a fact today that one in ten
thousand of us can make a technological breakthrough capable
of supporting all the rest. The youth of today are absolutely
right in recognizing this nonsense of earning a living.

We keep inventing jobs because of this false idea that everybody has to be employed at some kind of drudgery because,
according to Malthusian-Darwinian theory, he must justify his
right to exist. So we have inspectors of inspectors and people
making instruments for inspectors to inspect inspectors.

The true business of people should be to go back to school and
think about whatever it was they were thinking about before
somebody came along and told them they had to earn a living.

---

[42] This article in question can be found here < bit.ly/1gzBKPy >

DANIEL MILES: How astonishing that ideas expressed over 40 years ago, and at that time pretty much dismissed, should still be relevant today, in the sense that the main ideas are of course true, but also in the sense that those ideas have had essentially no impact whatsoever on human affairs. Again, because something does not suit the hegemony of our times, it is simply ignored. Value is determined by a thing's capacity to enrich the wealthy: if it fails on that measure, it is dismissed as useless. I see that Fuller's thoughts here in the symposium can be supported by the remark from Paul Ehrlich that follows directly after:

> Our economic growthmanship has trapped us. We have everybody working on a six-day treadmill and moonlighting so they can continue to cycle junk through their houses. We should find out how much gross national product the country really needs and try and produce it in the most relaxed, esthetic way possible. Substituting quality for quantity should apply to families, too. Any non-sterile moron can have twelve children.[43]

The best way to attack the notion that everyone must work is to point out that there are in fact two types of work. There is work that is required for the maintenance of human communities, and for enhancing the value that people find in their own

---

[43] Paul Ehrlich, biologist and educator, is best known for his warnings about population growth and limited resources (see his controversial 1968 book *The Population Bomb*). His general thesis is that the human population is too large, and is a direct threat to the environment and to the survival of humanity itself.

lives, which promotes in each the hope of advancing to the higher levels of Maslow's Hierarchy of Needs [see page 32]: this we can call productive work. Then there is stupid work. This is work that is pointless and useless, for it lacks any capacity to promote the satisfaction of Maslow's Needs, and perhaps diminishes the likelihood of such satisfaction. This is nonproductive work. People are forced to undertake it, and waste their lives on it, purely for the satisfaction of feeding the Profit Machine which churns out the wealth of the richest 1%, not, except in the rarest instances, to be used for the amelioration of the human condition, but for the pure indulgence of the 1% who claim ownership of all that which the 99% work to produce.

One key difficulty today seems to be the underlying, unquestioned assumption that all work, whatever its nature, is in and of itself something good. And there is the further assumption that whatever the work produces must also be something good. My favourite example is the initialled gearstick knob. This has got to be one of the most pointless, useless, valueless objects ever made by the ingenuity of human endeavour. The initialled gearstick knob is fundamentally stupid. It consumes raw materials, and it wears away the life of the person who makes it, day by day, until their blessed retirement comes, for an outcome that has no merit whatsoever. To use the initialled gearstick knob you have to throw away the perfectly good one that came with your car. So the production of the stupid initialled gearstick knob requires the destruction of the first one. This is one of the best examples of total, stupid, frippery that I have ever come across.

But, also, it is no more and no less symptomatic of how stupid the world is generally. For all commodities lie on a scale that has necessity at one end, and stupidity at the other. If the initialled gearstick knob is right at the stupid end, then the production of food will be right at the necessary end. Things that are necessary result from productive work, and stupid things result from stupid work.

Which brings us back to Ehrlich's question about how much of what is produced is really needed.

And brings us back to Fuller's question about how much of the *work* that is done is really needed. And *who* needs it to be done. For necessary and stupid work alike generate profit in the pockets of the 1%. It's all the same to them whether people grind out their lives on necessary work for necessary things, or on stupid work for stupid things. How can it be doubted that the Profit Machine requires the input of a massive quantity of stupid work if the wealthy are to be satisfied in their greed for ever more wealth? If only necessary things were to be produced, obviously the capitalist System would fall to pieces.

We should bear that in mind when we come to sum up what we think needs to happen for the present calamity to end. But having made the distinction between necessary work and stupid work, I think we should spend a little time on saying something about these two sorts of work, as well as give some thought to how much work we really need to do to provide for the entire community a descent standard of living - not in

terms of wages, but in terms of the products, goods and ser-
vices that are needed for basic comforts.

Well, necessary work attaches primarily to the things we
have to do to satisfy the basic needs at the very first level of
Maslow's Hierarchy of Needs [page 32] - biological and
physiological needs. Here we should list food, water, shelter,
clothing, sanitation and medical care. A civilised society
should also view as necessary the basic requirements for
security conceived in the most general of ways: so here we
should list emergency services, and the legal apparatus to
deal with criminals, but perhaps also those things required
for national security. It is no use building a civilised society
that is vulnerable to hostile people from outside. And there
will always be the need to be ready for natural disasters.

I was wondering about education. Is that not also essential,
although Maslow seems to include it only on level five of the
hierarchy?

Perhaps level five includes mostly academic education (if we
may speak loosely). Practical education is obviously a necessary component of the provisions required right down at
level one. No one can farm the land without possessing the
education that tells you how to actually do it. And so on. On
this view of what is required for a civilisation to flourish at
the most basic level, practical education will take a dominant position. I believe you have chanced upon some interesting material on the internet concerning the amount of
work that really needs to be done.

I have. At the economonitor.com site[44] I found a page where Ed Dolan looks at the question of necessary work,[45] and finds that only 13.7% of the economy is devoted to what he calls 'goods-producing industries' (which is something of a match for what we are calling 'necessary work') 'including mining, logging, manufacturing, and construction', to which he adds somewhere around 1.5 to 2% for farming, and comes up with the finding that only 15.5% of the economy is devoted to what we mean by 'productive' or 'necessary' work. Now, we don't have the expertise to make a proper assessment of this, but if this is anywhere near the truth of the matter, then about 85% of the economy is devoted to stupid work - to work that is not needed for sustaining a basic quality of life in a civilised society.

This is stupid work whose primary purpose is the enriching of the rich through the workings of the Profit Machine. Most of what most people do most of the time has absolutely nothing to do with what really needs to be done for the universal welfare of humankind, but is devoted to maintaining the lifestyles of the rich. What an almighty con! Is this really what culture and civilisation and science and technology come down to? Pampering the rich! I mean, what's going on

---

[44] 'The EconoMonitor brings together a community of economic, financial and geopolitical thinkers from around the world. Its purpose is to surface new ideas and to push forward the economic and geopolitical debate.'
[45] See the page here < bit.ly/1iBD8SN > His article deals with the economy of the USA, but we can suppose its findings apply equally well to all developed economies, include those of the UK and the European Union as a whole.

here? We have chanced upon this realisation somewhat late in life. Did we miss it the first time around? Does everyone know this, and simply accept it? It didn't occur to them that two silly old fools, you and me, needed to be told about this? How stupid can we have been!

Or perhaps we're all stupid, you and me and everyone else. Stupid or hoodwinked, or both. This is at least part of what it means to be a resource to be exploited, something of no real account that matters not in the least for any intrinsic quality it might have, like humanity, or creativity, or caring for people. If they could turn us all into robots, surely they would. And then we would have a planet owned by a few thousand incredibly rich people, served by seven billion robots whose main function is to provide for the rich humans, and make sure that the robots didn't break down - not for the benefit of the robots, but to ensure the presence of ever-flowing wealth and luxury into the laps of their owners.

I think we are back to slavery again...

I should add a bit more about Ed Dolan's discussion. He needs to extend his analysis to allow for the fact that much of what is consumed in the USA is manufactured in factories outside the country, including, for instance, China. This might suggest that his figure of 15.5% for how much productive work is needed is too low. He provides another analysis looking at GDP, exports and imports, and concludes that 'it would still only take 9 hours of our average 35-hour week to meet our demand for consumer goods in full'. That's about two hours a day in a five-day working week.[46]

So on this analysis, the proportion of stupid work seems to be about 75%. Not so different from the 85%. Wherever the truth lies, it lies in the fact that much, or even most of the work that is done in 'advanced' technological societies is in a fundamental sense *worthless*. It produces stuff that is not needed, not really, not on a more reasoned and morally nuanced perception of human welfare, that is, for the moment, swamped by the present dominion of profit-at-any-cost, so-long as the 1%-get-what-they-want.[47]

Let's go back and look at this from the other direction, not from the stupidity of the work that people do, but from the direction of the stupid things that all the stupid work produces. Let's give some substance to Ehrlich's remark about cycling junk through our houses.

---

[46] We accept that this sort of analysis is complex and demanding, and we cannot pretend we have mastered a full understanding. But what seems plain enough is that, without doubt, far too much work is done that simply does not need to be done. Far too much of this work is pointless to the point of stupidity, and far too much of it is implicated in the destruction of the global environment. It has only one purpose: to make rich people rich.

[47] As we were editing this chapter, we chanced upon David Graeber's article in *Strike! Magazine*, 'On the Phenomenon of Bullshit Jobs', in which he analyses the very same phenomenon we had been discussing. The 'bullshit job' that Graeber addresses appears to be the job someone wastes their life on, doing what we have called 'stupid work', work that provides no tangible benefit for anyone. The article can be found at the *Strike! Magazine* website, strikemag.org, here < bit.ly/18ZqQ39 >

We would urge our readers to watch this remarkable little animated documentary by Annie Leonard called *The Story of Stuff*.[48] The facts and figures that feature attach mostly to the economy of the USA, but its findings are applicable to all industrialised economies, including our own here in the UK, and across the European Union.

There is a wealth of material crammed into the 20 minutes that the video lasts, and we cannot pretend to do it proper justice in the few paragraphs we shall devote to it. But I think we can focus on three key notions that bear on the topic of our book.

Indeed. We should mention first the completely astonishing claim that in North America, looking at the whole materials economy sequence of resources extraction to production, to distribution, to consumption, to disposal, only one percent of the materials used are still in the hands of the consumer six months after purchase.[49] Virtually everything used in the production of any manufactured item is thrown away, and virtually every item produced by such waste is also thrown away, just months from the point at which it was taken out of its box which, of course, has also been thrown away. This

---

[48] This is available at storyofstuff.org. They have several videos: look for *The Story of Stuff*, or use this link < bit.ly/IPCL6M > A book under the same title was published in 2010 (see Bibliography).

[49] This is a reference to page 81 of *Natural Capitalism* by Paul Hawken, Amory Lovins and L. Hunter Lovins, published in 1999. To see Annie Leonard's notes and references for *The Story of Stuff*, see this PDF script available at her site < bit.ly/1nXDBPd >

must look to the aliens we imagined earlier [in Chapter 4], who are looking down trying to understand our world and what human beings are doing, that the whole purpose of industrial activity is to produce rubbish. The Profit Machine run by the rich for the benefit of the rich, at everyone else's expense, is in essence not much more than a rubbish spewing machine! When in exasperation someone complains that the modern world is crap, they are probably closer to the truth than they might imagine. The 1% treats the 99% as rubbish for the ultimate objective of producing rubbish!

There is a profound existential pointlessness to what the human race is doing...

Well, it wouldn't be so bad if existential pointlessness were the only problem. We should also mention the astonishing claim that one-third of the world's natural resources have already been used up[50]. This is truly alarming. Collectively, we are stealing from the future to have a blowout *now*. Not that you and I, nor 99% of the people whose views are disregarded when it comes to deciding corporate objectives, in any meaningful sense act collectively. No, it is the Profit Machine run for the benefit of the richest 1% that is gobbling up the natural resources that are thereby denied to future generations. The richest 1% of people is doing two things: they

---

[50] This is a reference to page 4 of *Natural Capitalism* (ibid). However accurate this assessment was then, the situation has obviously got a lot worse than that in the intervening years. If the true statistic is even remotely anywhere near this figure, human civilisation is in trouble.

are exploiting everyone who has to work in their global Profit Machine, and as we have explained, this is fairly represented as theft, and they are also stealing from future generations the resources for which we might guess *they themselves* would like to have responsibility. Well, that responsibility, on a day by day basis, is being stolen from them. They will not be able to make any decisions about how best to use their natural resources, because there won't be any left. Maybe they won't know what they're missing. If ancient peoples (let's say the Romans had had their own Industrial Revolution) had used up every last deposit of coal, every last drop of oil, we would not ourselves be able to have the sort of industries that we have.

Maybe that would be a good thing... We would never have known what we are missing, and without our own Industrial Revolution we may have been better off.

Maybe. But the point is that we would not have had the opportunity to exercise our own decisions in the matter. The Roman Industrial Revolution would have impoverished us today to at least this extent: decisions we have a right to, decisions about how to manage our world, whether or not to use natural resources, how much to use, and what to use them for, would have been taken away from us. We would not thank an earlier civilisation for depriving us in this way. But this is exactly what we are doing to future generations. We are *today* depriving them of their entitlements. The right to use natural resources is not exclusively ours. Of course, this question takes on a much bigger dimension when we consider other things such as global warming. Our use of natural resources *today* is wrecking the climate of the world tomorrow. That low-lying regions, many of them fertile farming areas, will be lost to future generations - whenever that might come about - *is our fault*. It is our fault now, and we have a moral responsibility to fix this catastrophe. But it won't happen, because making it happen does not profit the rich. 'So stuff future generations,' say the rich. 'Stuff the children of our children's children, and then stuff the children that will come after. Share prices are up today! Praise the mighty god of capitalism! Make the people of tomorrow yield up their sacrifices so that the richest 1% may live in luxury today! Let the ice-sheets melt for my benefit! My responsibility is to myself alone! Nothing else matters, not people, not my descendants, not the climate, not civilisation, not the planet itself! Praise be to profit!'

One feature of today's predicament which we have not really mentioned in so many words, and which comes out in striking fashion in Annie Leonard's video, is consumerism [the third key topic we will discuss]. Without the ideology of consumerism that promotes perpetual growth in the consumption of consumer goods, a major component of the Profit Machine would be left out of its flawed, fatal and grandiose design. If we think exploitation is the driving concept for the evil in the world today, consumerism must be its very close companion.

Well, consumerism is a sort of brainwashing technique, through which people are made to think that what is really benefiting the richest in society is in fact benefiting *them*. Of

course, when you buy a nice pair of shoes, and people com-
pliment you on your choice, you really do think that you are
in receipt of some kind of benefit. You do not even think in
terms of the profits being made from your choice, out of
your susceptibility to brainwashing, that drive up the value
of the shares owned by the 1%. That the rich, the corporations, the powerful and their friends, have purposefully and
systematically made every endeavour to trick people into
being good consumers cannot be doubted.[51] I think we
should include the words of Victor Lebow [economist and
retail analyst] included in *The Story of Stuff*. They expose
something deeply unpleasant about human beings, or at
least some human beings. These words connect to a patho-
logical materialism that seems to take itself seriously.[52]

> Our enormously productive economy demands that we make
> consumption our way of life, that we convert the buying and
> use of goods into rituals, that we seek our spiritual satisfactions,
> our ego satisfactions, in consumption. ... We need things con-
> sumed, burned up, worn out, replaced, and discarded at an ever
> increasing pace.[53]

---

[51] For more on this subject, we recommend most heartily the four-part
documentary series made by Adam Curtis in 2005, *The Century of the
Self*, available at the thoughtmaybe.com website < bit.ly/1kfn9tH >
[52] It is not clear whether Lebow was merely describing the nature of the
conspicuous consumption of his day, actively promoting it, or
alternatively using rhetorical effect to criticise it. See the message
thread at this blog < bit.ly/RKk5ua > for a discussion of this question.
[53] This is the shortened, edited, version that Annie Leonard includes in
her video. The full version obtained from Wikipedia < bit.ly/1gaLL6A >

This outlook, taken up enthusiastically over the intervening 60 years by those who control the Profit Machine, calling for the maximum possible rate of resources consumption, has been a complete catastrophe. What Lebow would not have known is that this outlook would, in little more than a generation, wreak havoc upon the planet's environment, and with evermore incremental success make the tiny, rich elite richer still, all at the expense of the humanity of the

---

comprising a larger text (containing the following two paragraphs) is from Victor Lebow's article 'Price Competition in 1955', in the Spring 1955 issue of *Journal of Retailing* < bit.ly/1ox9huM and bit.ly/TiDow3 > which discusses the cost of maintaining the American lifestyle in 1955, and the effect this cost had on retail profits:

Our enormously productive economy demands that we make consumption our way of life, that we convert the buying and use of goods into rituals, that we seek our spiritual satisfactions, our ego satisfactions, in consumption. The measure of social status, of social acceptance, of prestige, is now to be found in our consumptive patterns. The very meaning and significance of our lives today expressed in consumptive terms. The greater the pressures upon the individual to conform to safe and accepted social standards, the more does he tend to express his aspirations and his individuality in terms of what he wears, drives, eats - his home, his car, his pattern of food serving, his hobbies.

These commodities and services must be offered to the consumer with a special urgency. We require not only 'forced draft' consumption, but 'expensive' consumption as well. We need things consumed, burned up, worn out, replaced, and discarded at an ever increasing pace. We need to have people eat, drink, dress, ride, live, with ever more complicated and, therefore, constantly more expensive consumption. The home power tools and the whole 'do-it-yourself' movement are excellent examples of 'expensive' consumption.

unwitting 'slaves' of the Profit Machine which endlessly spews out rubbish, so it seems, as its primary purpose.

There is a sort of vicious cynicism at work here. At first sight, it might appear that consumerism offers each individual consumer the promise of having their desires fulfilled. Yet this is precisely what consumerism - understood as the public relations face of the Profit Machine that is trying to provoke people to spend their money on Stupid Goods created by Stupid Work - must never do. Were people to have their desires fulfilled, there would be no motive for buying yet more and more things. No. Consumer Propaganda must give the impression of offering satisfaction, but must in fact provoke people, continuously, into feeling the frustration of not having their desires fulfilled. Advertisements give the illusion that they are showing you what you might like to have in order to experience satisfaction of some sort, but their real purpose is to convince you that you are not satisfied by what you already have. The success of consumerism depends upon people being made as miserable as possible, to provoke them into action which they believe will relieve that misery. Yet no matter what they do, at all costs, that misery must remain at the core of their experience. It must be permanent and significant, ever ready to provoke the next purchase, and the purchase after that. This is like a craving that can never be satisfied, an addiction that demands to be fed, yet which can never be eased.

And that is another aspect of what we mean when we say that the capitalist System is using people as a resource to exploit for the benefit of the richest 1%. Your thought here suggests that the System works, or works better, when people are made to feel as miserable as possible. So, of course, we call this System evil, and this is why we say that evil lies at the heart of the capitalist System, because the pleasant lives experienced by the richest people can only be realised if the lives of the 99% are made unpleasant. And I find that disgusting. It nauseates me in a way I find hard to describe. Every time I see an advertisement on TV or in a magazine, I know that there are people out there seeing what I am seeing, and being made to feel miserable and inadequate, being made to feel unhappy with what they have. The whole bizarre spectacle is a complete con. And it hurts people.

The confidence trick manifests in the planned and perceived obsolescence that Annie Leonard mentions in her video.

Indeed. Why aren't consumers roused to outrage by this abuse? 'Planned obsolescence', where the designers and manufacturers deliberately work out how quickly they can make their products fail, is a downright abuse. Of course, we wouldn't need to go back for a replacement product if the first one didn't break or fail in some way.[54] Maybe most people are fooled into thinking that manufacturers really make every effort to make well-made and durable products, with the intention that they last as long as possible. Only very occasionally dare we think this is ever honestly attempted.

---

[54] Annie Leonard remarks: 'It means they actually make stuff that is designed to be useless as quickly as possible so we will chuck it and go buy a new one.'

You have a favourite example, I know.

I do. This is a product with the manufacturer's name ROLCUT engraved into the surface. My garden secateurs, which I have been using continuously since 1979, and which I have sharpened myself with a little hand-held tool only twice. As far as I can see, this manufacturer is no longer in business, probably because their products were too well made. I, for one, never needed to replace my secateurs. And here is one absurdity in the capitalist System. A manufacturer cannot make a good quality product because to do so would be to guarantee the eventual closure of the business. Once everyone who wants the thing they make has one, their sales figures will plummet. Their only hope is to continuously bring to the market new products. And again, I will feel dubious about the genuine need for this ever expanding range of products.

If the product doesn't fail, then the company that makes it will fail.

That's about the size of it. And the other sort of obsolescence, 'perceived obsolescence' is down to us. This is at least as disturbing as planned obsolescence, perhaps more so. For now, we don't throw something out because it has broken, necessitating the need to get a new one. No. We throw it out because we are in some way dissatisfied with it, even though it is functioning as well as ever. It has become outdated, gone out of fashion, it is old-looking; either it has a certain feature which newer models do not have (it has a button on the side instead of on the top), or it lacks a certain feature which the newer models have (the batteries don't last as long, or it is 4mm thicker); having an old one embarrasses us, makes us feel inadequate, makes us feel miserable. Now, I am struggling here to articulate this idea, because personally, I have never in my life cared anything whatsoever for what others might think of me for using something old, worn, out of date, or whatever. My secateurs are 35 years old; my car is 24 years old. I have shirts that date from the 1980s. As far as I can see, I am not in the least affected by 'perceived obsolescence' because I simply do not perceive it. For me, nothing can be obsolescent unless it has broken or failed. I believe I am immune to this aspect of the System's nonsense. But others, I can see, are not. And there is a shameful waste in this: a waste of resources, of manufacturing capacity, of the lives of the people who labour to make replacements for things that do not need replacing. This outrageous psychological manipulation of the population is perhaps the main impetus for Stupid Work, and this is just stupid. Well, it is more than that. It is vile in a sort of tragic way; it is disgusting and nauseating, because to feed the Profit Machine with its raw materials for the creation of Stupid Goods by Stupid Work all with the primary purpose of making rich people richer, the environment of the planet is being destroyed and, in consequence, a mass extinction is underway.[55] This makes humanity, the human species, collec-

---

[55] This from the mysterium.com website: 'If present trends continue one half of all species of life on earth will be extinct in less than 100 years, as a result of habitat destruction, pollution, invasive species, and climate

tively, a sort of lethal cancer feeding off the dying planet. And for that fact it deserves not to survive (and maybe it won't). We have no option but to redeem ourselves, if we can. The capitalist System must be replaced by something completely different; something that honours and promotes individual dignity and recognises and responds to the need for proper management of the planet. This need is truly desperate.

---

change.' < bit.ly/1jQmPlL > See also the *Wikipedia* 'Holocene extinction' article < bit.ly/1r6h8nN >

CAPITALISM

owner

consumer

minimum wage

profit

exploitation

zero-hours contract

investor

taxation

shareholder

worker

unemployment

inequality

environment

meritocracy

education

resources

MISERY & DESTRUCTION

HUMAN FLOURISHING

capitalism

socialism

anarchism

well-being

inequality

justice

democracy

autonomy

communism

human rights

environment

social security

population

universal basic income

health service

education

STEWARDSHIP OF THE PLANET

10

Dignity Restored

KARL GRUBER: *Is it possible for humanity to redeem itself, to alter our political and economic systems so radically that the paradise that could be here now will in short order actually arrive?*

DANIEL MILES: I am pessimistic, as you know. I think our enemy is too strong, and has a grip on our culture generally that will prove too powerful to throw off. The evil that is done through the workings of the capitalist System and its foul Profit Machine will end only with the arrival of evil on a completely different order of magnitude, when our current system collapses under the weight of the pressures which it is itself making more dangerous day by day. I am thinking here of soil erosion, the destruction of farmland, the worsening effects of global warming, over-fishing, contamination of food and water and of the environment generally, interruption of energy supplies, failure of the distribution system, epidemics and pandemics, and without doubt yet more banking and financial crises. Not to mention the wars. Resources depletion, and especially the competition for drinking water, will provoke violent reactions all over the globe - territorial claims, the rise of petty nationalisms and the seeking out of any available scapegoat will be the order of the day - the unemployed, the disabled, the immigrant, the asylum-seeker, the single mother. The real problems will go unmentioned, unperceived, unchallenged, whilst the 1% get richer and pay for armed guards to protect their gated communities, whilst the hell they have created to satisfy their greed descends upon and devours the 99% who will realise too late that it was they themselves who had been labouring to construct the prisons and slaughterhouses in which they now find themselves, whilst all the time continuing to believe the demonising rubbish written about them in the popular press.

This is the nightmare that I am not able to throw off.

Yet, even as the bus of total disaster bears the world's human population at breakneck speed towards the cliff edge, there will be some like you and me desperately trying to apply the break, whilst the lunatics who cannot see that there is anything wrong keep pulling us away, determined to let the driver carry on unimpeded. And in the midst of the commotion we will not know for sure whether the bus is in freefall, so we will keep on trying to apply the break. The frightening thought is that the bus might *already* be in freefall, and we simply don't know it.

But we don't know for sure. So we shout our warnings, and we protest our enslavement to the System, and we want an end to the evil, and we want a paradise for all, because we know at some instinctual level that human creativity and ingenuity and goodness of spirit can prevail. And here we are, discussing these problems...

Well, the enemy was certainly strong enough to brush aside the Occupy Movement, and by and large succeeded in ridiculing anyone who expressed sympathy for the protestors or who raised queries about the capitalist System.

As we remarked before [on pages 92-3], the protest movement could so easily be dismissed because, it could be claimed, if it had any representatives (and its appropriately abhorrent dislike for hierarchical structures suggested that it did not) - if anyone claimed to be speaking for the movement, their dismissal was a foregone conclusion because the framework within which any legitimate argument could be assessed had already been decided, or rather didn't even make it into conscious thought, because the unquestioned assumption that dominated any debate was that *capitalism was unchallengeable*. If, for instance, anyone complained about corruption, the response by journalists and commentators was to ask how the *present system* could be fixed; or if bankers' bonuses were criticised, the response was to ask how the *present banking system* could be changed.

This is a bit like the example of the windows in the pub that keep getting broken in bouts of drunken fighting, and the only plausible solution - it seems - is to fit stronger windows. Of course, the real solution is to cut the level of alcohol consumption and stop the fighting. But from the perspective of the publican's drive for profit, this solution cannot be conceived.

The framework of the discussion needs to be changed. The assumption that capitalism is the only game in town, and

VOTE FOR ONE CANDIDATE ONLY

1	**Peter James Smith** **PRO-CAPITALISM CANDIDATE** 120 Sudbury Court, Wembley, HA4 3TQ The Conservative Party	Conservatives
2	**Jane Sarah Brown** **PRO-CAPITALISM CANDIDATE** 2 Park East Place, London, W3 2PZ The Labour Party	Labour
3	**Paul William Jones** **PRO-CAPITALISM CANDIDATE** 15 Chiswell Park Avenue, London, EC2Y 7QY Liberal Democrats	Liberal Democrats
4	**Basil John Miller** **PRO-CAPITALISM CANDIDATE** 17 Chase Road, London, N24 7LD United Kingdom Independence Party	UKIP

that all its problems and all suggestions for solutions must therefore be confined to capitalism's continuation, must be thrown out.

This discussion about what the future will be like must be located in a completely different framework, in which capitalism is located amongst a wide range of ideas and concepts, all of which can claim an entitlement to feature in our deliberations. Of course, it is our view that capitalism features as a component in this larger framework in order to satisfy the requirement that it be wholly discarded. Capitalism is the fighting in the pub which if thrown out will prevent any more windows getting broken.[56]

The current disillusionment with politics stems from the rather obvious fact that politicians are simply failing to address the problems that people are really facing in the real world. And of course, the millionaire and multi-millionaire cabinet members of Prime Minister David Cameron's government have no interest in considering for a moment that the capitalist framework is itself at fault, and must be replaced. And so they are rightly seen as belonging to a privileged elite, out of touch with the realities of daily life, and they are rightly condemned for their stupidity and lack of humanity.

The political class put up their candidates at the elections, and what do they really offer us? It doesn't matter who you

---

[56] The concepts and ideas that we have placed within the different frameworks in our diagram on page 116 are of course not intended to be comprehensive.

vote for, because the outcome will inevitably be more capitalism. They offer policies that offer nothing that we want. They offer policies whose ultimate objective is to serve the interests of the richest 1%, that value profit over people, and show the way to a hateful future.

This is why political discourse must be reframed by different concepts and different objectives. All of our doings, the collective output and endeavour of the worldwide human community, must be directed at what really has value. And there is only one thing that has value, when seen in the most basic way possible. And that is the notion of flourishing - applied to everything - applied to the individual, to their family and community, but also to nature and the planet as a whole. The natural tendency for things to flourish has been undermined and ruined by the System. And it is getting so bad that, even were the System to be thrown down and replaced by something new and benign that fulfilled in an ideal way the needs of people and the needs of the planet, a full and complete recovery from the dire straits into which capitalism has pitched us could never be fully realised. In other words, we're stuffed. So we will have to get, no, demand what we want, and do our best to make what must be awful less awful than under the evil of capitalism.

That's as optimistic as I can get. I have an awful feeling that even if we can jam on the breaks of the bus of total disaster, all we will achieve is a screeching slither that results in the bus pitching over the cliff at one mile per hour. In the end, we will make no meaningful difference. I just hope I am wrong. So we will keep trying: talking and writing and speaking. We must wear ourselves out with effort.

What the System holds as its objective (making profit for the rich), and the means it employs to realise that objective (exploiting people and exploiting the natural world), are rightly regarded as evil because, put in the most basic terms, they inhibit or even destroy the capacity that both people and the planet as a whole have for flourishing. And by flourishing we mean that process by which anything achieves its ideal or perfected way of being in the world. The details for how any one person (a child at school, for instance) or how any one thing (a rainforest, for example) may flourish can be spelled out in detail and examined in the usual scientific manner, and such work is of course important. But for making progress in our discussion, I think we can rely upon an intuitive grasp of what flourishing means in any particular context. It is the destruc-

tion of flourishing, or at least its corruption, that we object to, and in this idea lies hope of finding solutions.

Indeed. This is the question that Maslow wanted to address with his Hierarchy of Needs - he is essentially asking, and offering answers to, the question: 'What is it for human beings to flourish?' And when we look at the sorts of options that political and economic systems are obligated to provide (in order not to end up the perpetrators of evil), and how we can summarise what a proper moral outlook must look like if the resources for flourishing are to be made available, we arrive at one simple concept: *dignity*. The present evil System may pay lip service to its weak grip on dignity by pointing out the extra chair that occasionally gets added to the stupid game of musical chairs [page 55] when the absurdity of social mobility is invoked, or when it grinds the nonsense of almost non-stop TV advertising into our retinas, saying that all we have to do to flourish (translating 'be happy', or 'be admired' or 'get more sex' or 'be envied by others') is buy this product, or wash our hair with that product, or feed this product to our cat. Or get a cat. Or run with cats...

Well, that is of course a distorted notion of what we think it is to flourish. The current materialistic, consumer society has a pretty wrong-headed notion of what flourishing is. One obviously dominate component of this, one that is obviously wrong, is that of being better than other people. We are in effect being told that if you are not better than other people, you will be miserable; if you are not superior to others in at least some ways, you will be despised. 'Earn more to be happy.'

'Own more to be happy.' 'Own more of what-others-cannot-afford to be happy.'

And of course, we know what must happen for our dignity to be restored. We must stop being exploited as mere components in the Profit Machine - stop being regarded and treated as a resource whose exploitation creates the profit that the System pipes directly into the bursting bank account of the 1%. We matter. Each of us matters. We matter as people who should not be struggling to overcome the obstacles that sprout up at every turn, as if they were connected to the very workings of the Profit Machine, so that as the wheels grind their inevitable revolutions, first this spring is released and unexpected unemployment shoots up and bars our way, then the next spring releases the slime of debt on us because the so-called safety-net of the Welfare State has been sadistically shredded by a Conservative Government intent on demonising its scapegoats and hoping to heap on them as much misery as is practically possible - so, of course, our social security payments, the payments that we have already paid for with our taxes, and to which we are entitled, are delayed or sanctioned through spite or some petty bureaucracy. Then we have to pay the Bedroom Tax; then the Council Tax goes up; then we are expected to take a job miles away, and commute for over four hours a day. Each of us will have our own story of how our dignity has been denied. And each of us will know the suffering that this brings. And each of us will know the futility of hope that remains forever disconnected from what actually happens to us. And we catch a glimpse of the paradise that should be here, yet is not. And we know it is not here because power is abused, because for those who wield power all that matters is the relentless operating of the Profit Machine. And we think *this stinks*. And we want something better - well, not so much better, as simply what we are entitled to from a technologically advanced culture whose functioning rests on sound and clear moral principles.

But there are no such principles.

No, only corrupted principles, only the hateful principles of exploitation and greed. Only the principle that wealth is right. Only the principle that all must be sacrificed on the Market's altar; and if that means another million children must be flung into poverty, well let's just hurl them into the pit![57]

And when we complain, they try to deceive us with musical chairs, and 'equal opportunities' and 'meritocracy' and 'capitalism cannot be challenged'.

So we return to our crushed dignity, and cradle it broken and weeping in our weary arms, and cry in bitter, angry tones, 'I'm not having this. This must stop. *I'm a human being, goddamn it; my life has value.*'[58]

---

[57] See footnote 17 for references to the topic of child poverty. See for instance the website at endchildpoverty.org.uk < bit.ly/1x3w3iX >
[58] The expression in italics is taken from the 1976 film, *Network*. See this at Wikipedia < bit.ly/1knDPAf >

We will include in an Appendix the text of the Universal Decla-
ration of Human Rights, because interestingly, this document
founds its analysis of human rights on the foundational notion
of dignity.[59]

We have taken a long time to discuss what is wrong with the
present system, and I think we should try to get more
specific about what the world would have to look like for our
DIGNITY to be restored. How we get from here to there, well,
that is not so easy to see, and here will lie any number of
obstacles set in our path by those who do not want us to
make the transition to a better future.

The most important quality possessed by dignity, it
seems to me, must be AUTONOMY.

The autonomous person decides, on the basis of their
own conscience and their own capacity to investigate the
nature of things, what objectives to have, and the means to
best pursue those objectives. In other words, they must be
able to decide freely what sort of person they want to be and
the things that this person will do. And they will do this from
a properly educated understanding of what gives value to a
human being, and what gives value to the sorts of things
that a human being can do and the sort of things that someone may seek to have populate their lives.

And what to value, in our present times, it seems must be
wealth and possessions and power.

---

[59] See the first paragraph of the Preamble, page 137.

Not that everyone actually adopts such a set of crude values by which to steer their course through life. Many people reject it, which is a good thing, but they reject it against the background, against a general attitude manifest everywhere, that indeed, only wealth and possessions and power are worth desiring. Anything else is at least a bit suspect, or worse than that, kooky. Is there not a general feeling abroad that non-material values are just a bit, well, silly?

Whatever such general attitudes might be, and how forceful their influence, the overarching objective must be the elimination of exploitation.

Of course, and it seems to me that there are three key solutions that go a very long way to eradicating this evil, almost overnight. The first would be to REDISTRIBUTE INCOME. The obscene income inequalities that we see in the world today, present in all nations and all cultures, cannot be sustained. It is, of course, nothing other than the manifestation of exploitation. Its presence establishes the fact of exploitation, the fact that some people are accorded an entitlement to the proceeds of the labour of others, a practice that we think is morally akin to direct slavery; and we mean that literally - there is no metaphor at work here. Just as the slave-owner owns their slaves with the express purpose of taking possession of what the labour of those slaves produces, and would, if they could forego maintaining their ownership of the slave's very body, but retain only their labour - well, so does the employer seek to take ownership of their employee's labour.

A fresh start for capitalism, then, would be to REDUCE INCOME INEQUALITY to a minimum. But the extent to which inequality is not wholly eliminated is the extent to which the immorality of exploitation still persists in the System, and thus it would remain an undesirable and unacceptable feature of contemporary society. Reducing the inequality would make what is very bad less bad than that, and could be accepted only as a stopgap whilst yet further changes are implemented. Yet, inequality is on the increase. It appears to be the desired end of capitalism, perhaps the very purpose of capitalism. And it appears to be the way of the sadist and the bully.

So we need more than that. We must wholly eliminate these inequalities. Our second solution is therefore that, eventually, all enterprises would become WORKER CO-OPERATIVES, in which each who contributes their labour - whatever their individual role might be - receives a wage at the very same hourly rate.[60] There are a variety of ways to set up co-operatives, but the key ideal seems to be WORKER PARTICIPATION, in which every co-worker contributes to

---

[60] This is more appropriately viewed as the ideal. Not all co-operatives pay workers the same basic rate. Insofar as co-operatives are set up to pursue the aspiration of equality, unequal pay seems to undermine the most important objective. Though, a pay scale based on length of service is perhaps not unacceptable. See this at the *Guardian* website < bit.ly/1pPS96z > where we are told: 'Of course equity is one of our co-operative values, so all co-operatives would subscribe to equal pay for equal work. However many co-operatives do have pay scales and pay differentials, some following the example of the famous Spanish co-operative Mondragon by limiting differentials between managerial and shop-floor workers' pay.'

the management processes through which the enterprise receives its objectives and by which these objectives are accomplished, but also manages how the profits of the enterprise will be distributed.[61] Of course, other considerations must be discussed, not least the question of how such enterprises receive their start-up cash; if, as in the present capitalist System an investor can buy shares which entitles them to some of the output generated by the workers' labour, then we have not done enough the solve the evil inherent in the System. So some other alternative must be adopted.

And the third solution?

I have left the best till last. This is the solution that can be implemented right now, without making any other significant changes to the capitalist System. It leaves the fundamental questions of exploitation and gross inequality (for the moment) unaddressed. But it offers what I think is a profound moral improvement, and this is the notion of providing for each and every citizen, as a matter of right, a UNIVERSAL BASIC INCOME, which is also referred to as *unconditional basic income, basic income guarantee,* or more simply just as *basic income.*[62]

---

[61] See the *Wikipedia* 'Worker Cooperative' article < bit.ly/1rVM8Y9 > and see especially the books by Richard Wolff which we list in the Bibliography.
[62] For a basic introduction, see the *Wikipedia* 'Basic Income' article < bit.ly/18yy5cz > and the 'Guaranteed Minimum Income' article < bit.ly/1n659Sk >

And this basic income would be set at a level sufficient at least for the bare minimum of survival, sufficient for the basic requirements of food and shelter, sufficient that is to provide for the most basic level on Maslow's Hierarchy [page 32]?

Yes, indeed. This measure directly and immediately extends to everyone a robust and foundational dignity. It makes as it were a declaration: you are the product of this civilisation, and as such, in virtue of your qualities as a human being, and in virtue of the rights that a civilisation worthy of being called such must extend to you, you are gifted this basic resource. You are hereby granted the capacity [at least in some small, but meaningful and worthwhile measure] to make of your life what you will. You may contribute as you wish. You may work in this or that enterprise, or be self-employed; you may learn, you may create, you may care for others or care for children; you may teach, you may research; you may sit back and simply observe the antics of the world with no particular objective in mind at all. Or you may combine your preferences in any way you wish.[63]

Such a declaration recognises something that has profound value, the capacity for independent, free agency - that is, the capacity to act however one so chooses - that each and every human being possesses, that lies at the very core of our self-conscious experience. Most importantly of all, it allows us to choose not to suffer the indignity of being

---

[63] An internet search will locate many interesting sites that discuss the idea of the basic income. See for instance the basicincome.org.uk website < bit.ly/1kCowoO >

make poverty history

BASIC INCOME

**A Basic Income (or Citizen's Income or Guaranteed Income)
is an automatic, unconditional and nonwithdrawable
income for every citizen and is NOT linked to work.**

**A Basic Income is rooted in the principle that
the world is the common property of us all.**

**In his final book "Where Do We Go from Here:
Chaos or Community?" (1967) Martin Luther King Jr. wrote
"I am now convinced that the simplest approach will
prove to be the most effective — the solution to poverty
is to abolish it directly by a now widely discussed measure:
the guaranteed income."**

**GOOGLE "BASIC INCOME" FOR MORE INFORMATION
AND TO FIND OUT HOW YOU CAN GET INVOLVED**

exploited by the capitalist System. We would no longer be compelled, in the manner of slaves, to provide for the life-styles of the richest 1%.

Indeed, any culture, society or government that does not recognise this connection between the basic entitlement of the guaranteed basic income and our freedom to choose, in the most thoroughgoing manner imaginable as the foundation of human flourishing, should be deemed invalid, and its authority to govern, or in any sense structure the lives of human beings, denied.

This is the state of affairs at this moment of history. We are part of an awakening of consciousness which realises the invalidity of the capitalist System and flinches at the evil it inflicts, and which declares, in this revelatory moment of insight and in the presence of truth, *no more.*

There are other components to our vision of a better future, a future that has done away with exploiting people and the natural world, acknowledged in the Universal Declaration of Human Rights. And to this extent we view the Declaration as a blueprint for what we want the future to be.

It is important to recognise that the Declaration is not the end of the process, but the beginning of a work in progress. It sets out as a bare minimum the standards that are acceptable for any government to claim legitimacy to rule its people. Should this bare minimum be satisfied, then we are ready to move on to the next stage and find out what comes next on our road to a paradise for all, because this paradise is a birth-right possessed of all human beings, the denial of which is a denial of our very humanity. Here is another perspective from which we can conclude that capitalism is an evil: it denies our humanity and treats us as chattels.

The idea that incomes should be made more equal is intimated in Article 23, and the ideal that everyone is entitled to a universal basic income is manifest in at least rudimentary form in Articles 22.2, 22 and 25.1.

But other UNIVERSAL ENTITLEMENTS are also arguably hinted at: that we should all have access to UNIVERSAL EDUCATION at any stage of life as a matter of entitlement is suggested by Articles 26 and 27, as are universal entitlements of all sorts, especially entitlements to MEDICAL CARE, HOUSING, CLOTHING, FOOD, LEISURE, and whatever may be deemed necessary to provide for SOCIAL SECURITY generally, in Articles 3, 22, 23, 24 and 25.

As we wind up our work for this book and prepare for publication, we find in the news something so crass and nasty, so abhorrent to the sanctity of human personhood and agency, that we can hardly believe it. This is the news that the Conservative government has pledged, if re-elected, to scrap human rights legislation.[64]

This is ostensibly a measure to deal with problems around immigration, and it seems clear that being able to stoke up fears and bigotries about immigrants has been carefully prepared to deny to everyone their human rights, when it suits

---

[64] See this at the *Guardian* < bit.ly/1cmALz9 >

a government whose objective is satisfying the interests of the 1%, the rich, the privileged, the powerful.

Such an approach, an approach which in all matters serves the 1%, *does not serve our interests*, the interests, needs and entitlement of the 99%. We do not want that.

We want an economic, financial, social and cultural system that works for our advantage, for the advantage of all, not just the few. And we want a system that nurtures rather than destroys, that instead of exploiting, causes everything to flourish.

The views that a society is flourishing only if GDP is rising is cretinous and dangerous. It is the understanding of fools, dangerous fools. Habitats, cultures, peoples have been trampled underfoot and tossed aside for the benefit of the richest few who have the power to satisfy their own interests at the expense of everyone and everything else.

What an utterly disgusting notion it is, that someone's worth has to be interpreted, realised and valued only in terms of the value that their labour has to someone who thinks that they *own* the proceeds of that labour, even if today they do not necessarily think that they own the labouring person themselves.

What an utterly disgusting notion it is that the 'health' of the economy takes precedence over the health of individuals - that the metaphor of 'economic health' should matter out of all proportion to the lives of the people who provide the labour as the fuel the economy must burn to keep functioning.

What an utterly disgusting notion it is that how well people are flourishing should be calculated primarily in terms of what they earn (which really means what they can make for those who own their labour).

'Look,' they cry, 'we have decimated forests, ruined environments; we have belching factories and filthy air; we have damaged communities, uprooted children, and we have precarity on a massive scale; we have food banks and a despised underclass of skivers. And you dare to object to our fine achievement! So what are you going to put in its place, eh? Tell us that!'

Well, I think we just did tell them. Now we will await the response of our Masters, but I don't think we are going to be surprised at the evil they will continue to serve up, to keep us in our place as their servants.

Appendix

Universal Declaration of Human Rights

Preamble

Whereas recognition of the inherent dignity and of the equal and inalienable rights of all members of the human family is the foundation of freedom, justice and peace in the world,

Whereas disregard and contempt for human rights have resulted in barbarous acts which have outraged the conscience of mankind, and the advent of a world in which human beings shall enjoy freedom of speech and belief and freedom from fear and want has been proclaimed as the highest aspiration of the common people,

Whereas it is essential, if man is not to be compelled to have recourse, as a last resort, to rebellion against tyranny and oppression, that human rights should be protected by the rule of law,

Whereas it is essential to promote the development of friendly relations between nations,

Whereas the peoples of the United Nations have in the Charter reaffirmed their faith in fundamental human rights, in the dignity and worth of the human person and in the equal rights of men and women and have determined to promote social progress and better standards of life in larger freedom,

Whereas Member States have pledged themselves to achieve, in co-operation with the United Nations, the promotion of universal respect for and observance of human rights and fundamental freedoms,

Whereas a common understanding of these rights and freedoms is of the greatest importance for the full realization of this pledge,

Now, therefore,
The General Assembly,
proclaims this
Universal Declaration of Human Rights

as a common standard of achievement for all peoples and all nations, to the end that every individual and every organ of society, keeping this Declaration constantly in mind, shall strive by teaching and education to promote respect for these rights and freedoms and by progressive measures, national and international, to secure their universal and effective recognition and observance, both among the peoples of Member States themselves and among the peoples of territories under their jurisdiction.

Article 1

All human beings are born free and equal in dignity and rights. They are endowed with reason and conscience and should act towards one another in a spirit of brotherhood.

Article 2

Everyone is entitled to all the rights and freedoms set forth in this Declaration, without distinction of any kind, such as race, colour, sex, language, religion, political or other opinion, national or social origin, property, birth or other status.

Furthermore, no distinction shall be made on the basis of the political, jurisdictional or international status of the country or territory to which a person belongs, whether it be independent, trust, non-self-governing or under any other limitation of sovereignty.

Article 3

Everyone has the right to life, liberty and the security of person.

Article 4

No one shall be held in slavery or servitude; slavery and the slave trade shall be prohibited in all their forms.

Article 5

No one shall be subjected to torture or to cruel, inhuman or degrading treatment or punishment.

Article 6

Everyone has the right to recognition everywhere as a person before the law.

Article 7

All are equal before the law and are entitled without any discrimination to equal protection of the law. All are entitled to equal protection against any discrimination in violation of this Declaration and against any incitement to such discrimination.

Article 8

Everyone has the right to an effective remedy by the competent national tribunals for acts violating the fundamental rights granted him by the constitution or by law.

Article 9

No one shall be subjected to arbitrary arrest, detention or exile.

Article 10

Everyone is entitled in full equality to a fair and public hearing by an independent and impartial tribunal, in the determination of his rights and obligations and of any criminal charge against him.

Article 11

1. Everyone charged with a penal offence has the right to be presumed innocent until proved guilty according to law

in a public trial at which he has had all the guarantees necessary for his defence.

2. No one shall be held guilty of any penal offence on account of any act or omission which did not constitute a penal offence, under national or international law, at the time when it was committed. Nor shall a heavier penalty be imposed than the one that was applicable at the time the penal offence was committed.

Article 12
No one shall be subjected to arbitrary interference with his privacy, family, home or correspondence, nor to attacks upon his honour and reputation. Everyone has the right to the protection of the law against such interference or attacks.

Article 13
1. Everyone has the right to freedom of movement and residence within the borders of each state.

2. Everyone has the right to leave any country, including his own, and to return to his country.

Article 14
1. Everyone has the right to seek and to enjoy in other countries asylum from persecution.

2. This right may not be invoked in the case of prosecutions genuinely arising from non-political crimes or from acts contrary to the purposes and principles of the United Nations.

Article 15

1. Everyone has the right to a nationality.

2. No one shall be arbitrarily deprived of his nationality nor be denied the right to change his nationality.

Article 16

1. Men and women of full age, without any limitation due to race, nationality or religion, have the right to marry and to found a family. They are entitled to equal rights as to marriage, during marriage and at its dissolution.

2. Marriage shall be entered into only with the free and full consent of the intending spouses.

3. The family is the natural and fundamental group unit of society and is entitled to protection by society and the State.

Article 17

1. Everyone has the right to own property alone as well as in association with others.

2. No one shall be arbitrarily deprived of his property.

Article 18

Everyone has the right to freedom of thought, conscience and religion; this right includes freedom to change his religion or belief, and freedom, either alone or in community with others and in public or private, to manifest his religion or belief in teaching, practice, worship and observance.

Article 19

Everyone has the right to freedom of opinion and expression; this right includes freedom to hold opinions without interference and to seek, receive and impart information and ideas through any media and regardless of frontiers.

Article 20

1. Everyone has the right to freedom of peaceful assembly and association.

2. No one may be compelled to belong to an association.

Article 21

1. Everyone has the right to take part in the government of his country, directly or through freely chosen representatives.

2. Everyone has the right of equal access to public service in his country.

3. The will of the people shall be the basis of the authority of government; this will shall be expressed in periodic and genuine elections which shall be by universal and equal suffrage and shall be held by secret vote or by equivalent free voting procedures.

Article 22

Everyone, as a member of society, has the right to social security and is entitled to realization, through national effort and international co-operation and in accordance with the organization and resources of each State, of the economic, social and cultural rights indispensable for his dignity and the free development of his personality.

Article 23

1. Everyone has the right to work, to free choice of employment, to just and favourable conditions of work and to protection against unemployment.

2. Everyone, without any discrimination, has the right to equal pay for equal work.

3. Everyone who works has the right to just and favourable remuneration insuring for himself and his family an existence worthy of human dignity, and supplemented, if necessary, by other means of social protection.

4. Everyone has the right to form and to join trade unions for the protection of his interests.

Article 24

Everyone has the right to rest and leisure, including reasonable limitation of working hours and periodic holidays with pay.

Article 25

1. Everyone has the right to a standard of living adequate for the health and well-being of himself and of his family, including food, clothing, housing and medical care and necessary social services, and the right to security in the event of unemployment, sickness, disability, widowhood, old age or other lack of livelihood in circumstances beyond his control.

2. Motherhood and childhood are entitled to special care and assistance. All children, whether born in or out of wedlock, shall enjoy the same social protection.

Article 26

1. Everyone has the right to education. Education shall be free, at least in the elementary and fundamental stages. Elementary education shall be compulsory. Technical and professional education shall be made generally available and higher education shall be equally accessible to all on the basis of merit.

2. Education shall be directed to the full development of the human personality and to the strengthening of respect for human rights and fundamental freedoms. It shall promote understanding, tolerance and friendship among all nations, racial or religious groups, and shall further the activities of the United Nations for the maintenance of peace.

3. Parents have a prior right to choose the kind of education that shall be given to their children.

Article 27

1. Everyone has the right freely to participate in the cultural life of the community, to enjoy the arts and to share in scientific advancement and its benefits.

2. Everyone has the right to the protection of the moral and material interests resulting from any scientific, literary or artistic production of which he is the author.

Article 28

Everyone is entitled to a social and international order in which the rights and freedoms set forth in this Declaration can be fully realized.

Article 29

1. Everyone has duties to the community in which alone the free and full development of his personality is possible.

2. In the exercise of his rights and freedoms, everyone shall be subject only to such limitations as are determined by law solely for the purpose of securing due recognition and respect for the rights and freedoms of others and of meeting the just requirements of morality, public order and the general welfare in a democratic society.

3. These rights and freedoms may in no case be exercised contrary to the purposes and principles of the United Nations.

Article 30

Nothing in this Declaration may be interpreted as implying for any State, group or person any right to engage in any activity or to perform any act aimed at the destruction of any of the rights and freedoms set forth herein.

Bibliography

Badiou, Alain. 2012. *The Rebirth of History: Times of Riots and Uprisings*. London: Verso.

Barlow, Elizabeth. 1970. New York Environmental Teach-In. *New York* 3-13, March 1970, 24-30 < bit.ly/1gzBKPy >

Benn, Tony. 2009. *Letters to my Grandchildren: Thoughts on the Future*. London: Hutchinson.

Castells, Manuel. 2012. *Networks of Outrage and Hope: Social Movements in the Internet Age*. Cambridge: Polity Press.

Cohen, G. A. 2009. *Why Not Socialism?* Princeton: Princeton University Press.

Duffy, Simon. 2013. *A Fair Society? How the Cuts Target Disabled People*. Sheffield: Centre for Welfare Reform.

Fisher, Mark. 2009. *Capitalist Realism: Is There No Alternative?* Winchester: Zero Books.

Graeber, David. 2013. On the Phenomenon of Bullshit Jobs. *Strike! The Summer of … Issue,* Summer 2013, 10-11 < bit.ly/18ZqQ39 >

Graeber, David and Barbara Jacobson. 2013. Unconditional Basic Income. Occupy London TV < bit.ly/1xiadbR >

Hessel, Stéphane. 2011. *Time for Outrage!* trans. Damion
    Smith and Alba Arrikha. London: Charles Glass. [First
    published in France in 2010 as *Indignez-vous!*]
——— . 2012. *The Power of Indignation: The Autobiography of
    the Man Who Inspired the Arab Spring*. trans. E. C. Belli.
    New York: Skyhorse.
Hessel, Stéphane and Edgar Morin. 2012. *The Path to Hope*.
    trans. Antony Shugaar. New York: Other Press. [First
    published in France in 2011 as *Le chemin de l'espérance*.]
Invisible Committee. 2009. *The Coming Insurrection*. Los An-
    geles: Semiotext(e).
Jameson, Fredric. 2003. Future City. *New Left Review* 21,
    May-June 2003, 65-79 < bit.ly/TlDUAX >
Judt, Tony. 2010. *Ill Fares the Land: A Treatise on Our Present
    Discontents*. London: Penguin.
Leonard, Annie. 2010. *The Story of Stuff*. London: Constable
    & Robinson. See her short video presentation at storyof
    stuff.org < bit.ly/IPCL6M >
Mander, Jerry. 2012. *The Capitalism Papers: Fatal Flaws of an
    Obsolete System*. Berkeley, CA: Counterpoint.
Maslow, Abraham. 1943. A Theory of Human Motivation.
    Psychological Review 50, 1943, 370-96 < bit.ly/hr7BR >
Mason, Paul. 2013. *Why It's Still Kicking Off Everywhere*. Lon-
    don: Verso.
McMurtry, John. 2013. *The Cancer Stage of Capitalism: From
    Crisis to Cure*. London: Pluto Press.
Raventós, Daniel. 2007. *Basic Income: The Material Condi-
    tions of Freedom*. London: Pluto Press.
Richards, Vernon. ed. 1983. *Why Work? Arguments for the
    Leisure Society*. London: Freedom Press.

Ronson, Jon. 2011. *The Psychopath Test*. London: Picador.

Stout, Martha. 2005. *The Sociopath Next Door*. New York: Broadway Books.

Taylor, J. D. 2013. *Negative Capitalism: Cynicism in the Neoliberal Era*. Winchester: Zero Books.

Tormey, Simon. 2013. *Anti-Capitalism: A Beginner's Guide*. London: Oneworld.

Torry, Malcolm. 2013. *Money for Everyone: Why We Need a Citizen's Income*. Bristol: Polity Press.

Virilio, Paul. 2012. *The Administration of Fear*. Los Angeles: Semiotext(e).

Wolff, Richard. 2012. *Democracy at Work: A Cure for Capitalism*. Chicago: Haymarket Books.

Wolff, Richard, in conversation with David Barsamian. 2012. *Occupy the Economy*. San Francisco: City Lights.

Žižek, Slavoj. 2009a. *First as Tragedy, Then as Farce*. London: Verso.

——. 2009b. *Violence*. London: Profile Books.

——. 2011. *Living in the End Times*. revised paperback edition. London: Verso. [Contains a new, 80-page Afterword.]

——. 2012. *The Year of Dreaming Dangerously*. London: Verso.

——. 2013. *Demanding the Impossible*. ed. Yong-june Park. Cambridge: Polity Press.

THIS IS OUR COUNTRY
WE WILL OCCUPY IT
THESE ARE OUR STREETS
WE WILL OCCUPY THEM
WE ARE HERE. WE ARE GROWING.

WE ARE THE
99%

OCCUPY **TOGETHER**

#OccupyWallSt #OccupyTogether occupytogether.org occupywallst.org

Outtakes, Extras and Alternative Ending

When you make a book from a long series of recorded conversations, you inevitably end up with a great many outtakes littering the cutting-room floor. Some merely repeated the material that was chosen for the final cut, and some simply refused to fit into the flow of the discussion as we shaped it for the printed page. Here is a selection of the bits we didn't want to throw away. Most have been retained in this little appendix because they contain a turn of phrase that we like or an oblique way of looking at something around which new discussions can grow. Some are simply outrageously polemical. As before, my words are in italics, and Daniel's are in roman type.

— Karl Gruber

Since the 1970s, capitalism has proved spectacularly successful at making a tiny elite spectacularly rich whilst presiding over an even more spectacularly widening gulf between rich and poor. On other measures (witness the pile of crises presented in our Introduction) capitalism has failed spectacularly. It has become a threat to humanity and a threat to the planet as a whole.

In very broad strokes, the dangerous monster that is capitalism has flourished and grown bigger because of one overriding principle that governs its modus operandi. And that is not just its willingness, but its mandatory exploitation of 99% of the human population, together with its rapacious appropriation of the natural resources that feed its appetite.

Everything they make you do hastens global destruction.

The capitalist cares nothing about you, *absolutely nothing.* They do not care whether you are happy or miserable, well or ill, fulfilled or frustrated. They don't even care that you are alive rather than dead. You mean *absolutely nothing* to them. The only interest they have in you, should you live a little longer, is whether they can get you to do the work that will - together with all the effort from other people whom they also care nothing for - furnish them with their multimillionaire lifestyles. Whether or not you will ever catch them sneering at you for not being rich, or not being devious enough to work the exploiter's trick to reap the benefit of greed at the expense of those who must serve your interests, well, you will have to decide that for yourself.

You mean as little to them as a cog in a machine, or a byte of information moving inside a computer.

They don't even care if you have enough to eat. Food banks can take care of that problem (because, of course, there is no problem here *for them*). But notice how some of them, just wait and bide your time, and keep on looking - how some of them will blame the plight of those dependent on food banks on the dependents themselves, and further, suggest that there is something unsavoury, something fishy about the person who sets out to fleece the food bank as if they are out to get something from others to which they are not entitled. The exploiters will cast the aspersion of exploiter on those they exploit. Look for their smug, self-satisfied expression of disgust; listen for the vehemence they can hardly contain when they condemn the person dependent on the food bank.

In superhero comics there is always some precipitating event, usually an accident, that exposes the yet-to-be hero to some sort of toxin or radiation, that in the real world would prove fatal, but which in the comic confers a superpower by which the superhero's status is recognised and by which their project to rid the world of some evil can be realised.

Our witnessing the riots in London and other urban centres in the summer of 2011 had a similar effect on Daniel and me.

There is one dominant belief or outlook that drives the neoliberal capitalist agenda, and this is the belief that it is appropriate and acceptable to exploit resources of all sorts, including human beings, otherwise known by a term reserved for bees and ants - workers. Their status as individuals is utterly ignored, utterly dismissed as having no more relevance than the status of this insect or that insect.

We live in a time of bizarre normalisations, where what is horrific or nasty, or brutal or mean, is accepted as normal. It is now normal to be kettled by anxieties, hemmed in by fear, sanctioned by terror, victimised for poverty.

If you receive more than the median income, then you are making a net gain from the exploitative System: the extent to which you are receiving less is the extent to which you are working, not for your own benefit, but for the benefit of the rich, as someone purposefully exploited, deliberately taken advantage of, as someone bullied and beaten to the exploiter's will. At other times in history, this arrangement was called slavery. Today it is called capitalism. Tomorrow, I hope (with a detestation that is hard to describe) - tomorrow, I hope it will be called barbaric, and its immorality will be repugnant to everyone.

Imagine that for a month, you suffer from a strange illness, rendering everything you do a sort of dream. You go out, go to work, do things, but as in a dream, you have no real understanding of what you are doing or why. At the end of the month, your mental faculties return to normal, and now you can see exactly what it is you have been doing; and now you can see whether you have been exploited or whether you have been enjoying a standard of living as someone who exploits, supported by the work of people poorer than you.

What would you rather be? Exploiter or exploited? Why choose one answer but not the other? Aren't both equally unacceptable?

The long and short of it is that capitalism is destroying the planet. Our choice is not so much between deciding which economic and social system we will live under, but whether we choose to save the planet or let the rapacity of capitalism shut off all options apart from squalor, war, deprivation and the despotism of the 1%. And until capitalism is ended, those children who are abused by the System, when they are old enough to understand the horrors and injustices that erode their well-being, should rail against their parents and grandparents and great-grandparents demanding to know why the desires of billionaires and millionaires should, after all this time still take precedence over their most basic needs. For this much society owes them in virtue of their being human children - a full recognition of what their basic needs are, and why they have been denied.

The Conservative-led coalition is too incompetent at running the economy to provide a good life for everyone, and instead finds ways to appropriate the efforts of the many, but disadvantaged poor, for the benefit of the wealthy elite and their slightly less wealthy friends. Ours is thus truly a plutocracy - a society ruled by the rich for the benefit of the rich. This being so, the rest of us are no more than their servants, needed only for the service we provide in their endeavour, otherwise surplus to requirements, ready to be pilloried and demonised as scroungers if we do not work all the hours that God gives in the pursuit of profit for the rich elite.

There is just one particular crisis that needs to be addressed - the crisis-of-what-the-blazes-can-we-do-about-all-these-crises? This is the crisis of not knowing what to do, whilst being certain that something must be done. What we require is a profound, visceral grip on what the *overarching crisis* actually is. *It is the fact of exploitation.*

One sort of evil arises when good is absent, as when the good of sound health is absent, and someone endures the ending of former good health. Good and evil can thus be seen as opposing dispositions which more or less stay in balance. But then there is absolute evil, an evil for which there is no counterbalancing good, when there is nothing whose arrival could remove the evil.

This is the evil of the capitalist System of organising our affairs, an evil whose presence is a necessary condition for the working of the System. There is no good that the capitalists might toss our way that can counterbalance the evil. The capitalist System itself is evil, absolutely evil. The evil must be present, always, permanently, for everyone who serves the System and for the System to exist at all. It is predicated on an ideal of abuse, and all but those who command the System must suffer it. We cannot seek an ending to this abuse within the System itself, because the evil is absolute. It is not possible to replace evil abuse by good abuse, since all abuse is necessarily evil. Whilst the System exists, evil exists absolutely.

These crises do not involve just the procedures by which human beings organise their politics, cultural and economic activities, but also directly affect the natural world which ultimately supports all our activities. If that were not the case - if our problems really were confined to our own petty affairs independently of environmental degradation and destruction, perhaps things really wouldn't be that bad. No matter how awful things get, we can always think that at another time there will be people who can try this again, who may succeed in creating a genuinely just society within

which people can lead genuinely fulfilling lives. But this possibility is itself being destroyed.

*One of the fundamental principles by which our society is
structured is inequality. This is patently the case, and is
proved by the fact that for 30 years or more, the wealthiest
people whose power controls the flow of events have striven,
and succeeded, to make inequality more and more extreme.
Some few live at the extremes of luxury whilst many more suffer the indignity of the queue outside the food bank, and the
scorn of the wealthy which casts such people as the authors of
their own plight.*

*Other principles we should consider are power, wealth,
materialism, exploitation, consumerism - and we see them at
work in the control, repression, and discrimination of the 99%
who labour for the benefit of the 1%.*

The problem, in essence, is a simple one. Stupid people believe stupid things, and when those stupid people have the
power to pursue policies predicated on their stupid beliefs,
sooner rather than later, evil will result. Worse still is the
stupid person who has power, and who is also evil, with
scores to settle, jealousies to avenge, and ideologies to im-
pose.

*How do you respond to the charge that rage is pure negativity,
something destructive and counter-productive?*

It depends on what has stimulated the rage and what it is
directed at. Thus rage can be justified, its attitude supported

by evidence and argument. It can be the end product of a careful process of analysis and thought. What matters is the context of the rage, not just *that it is rage*, but why it stirred into activity in the first place. This, I think is the purpose of our book, to examine the content of our rage and explore the arguments that explain its existence, and offer solutions for its remedy.

It is important to emphasise *solutions* in the plural. There are many things that are wrong, whether more or less integrated with the other wrong things, and there are many solutions, there are different ways to do things that in being different are not wrong any more, and there are new ways to do things that have not been done before, whose realisation can replace or surmount what is wrong.

We require solutions because, without question, much is wrong: climate change, destruction of the natural environment, species extinction. Connected to these issues in fundamental ways are questions concerning, what should we call it? - *human affairs* - questions concerning politics, economics, the way we treat each other, our motives and ideals, and ultimately our choices to work to build a better world for all, or only for some, and for some to strive only for their individual advantage to the detriment of collective well-being.

How do we get this across? What is happening is *bad*. So our rage should be enormous. It should sweep over and sweep up all the things that are wrong. The extinction of even a single species, no matter what it is, is a loss that can never be made good. The only reasonable response to all these calamities that we can mention is rage. We should howl our fury that power promotes destruction, that in pursuing its own selfish ends, power promotes misery for everyone else. We should rage against inequalities and a System which makes possible and even promotes the fewest number of people having incomes that are thousands of times larger than the subsistence wages of the poorest.

What could have been a beautiful world, a paradise for all, has been made nasty for the benefit of the few, who value their profit as more important than the health of the natural world or the well-being of their fellow man. Oh yes. We should rage against all these things.

Some people, usually wealthy people, who resent paying tax cannot stand the fact that 'their' wealth goes to pay the benefit payments of poor workers, single parents, the unemployed, the sick and disabled. But should we not ask in response, who really benefits from the capitalist System?

Those who benefit most are those who enjoy the greatest wealth, obviously. Yet the fact that their wealth, the *benefit* that they receive from the way society organises its affairs, is made for them in factories, workshops, call-centres and shops by ordinary workers on low wages, minimum wages, or on zero-hours contracts is hardly mentioned. Yet *they* feel hard done by? It is as if the plans for the Profit Machine by whose function the wealthy get everyone to work for their wealth must be kept secret, because it is something shameful, and discussing it openly must be avoided at all costs.

The shame is real and condemning. The existence of even a single child living in poverty, deprived of basic necessities and comforts taken for granted by the rich, in a technologically advanced society ranked as one of the richest in the world, verges on the criminal.

This is not the world that my grandfather fought for in the Second World War; it is not the world for which so many sacrificed their lives to defeat a horrid, horrid evil; no, it has become that horrid evil itself. The evil is here, now, at work in our midst, making couples row and children weep; it laps at the doors of the food banks and it saps the humanity from us all. Maybe it tries to justify itself in the smiling mask of the consumer society, in baubles and shiny things, in consumer goods, in pointless gadgets, designed to entice us and trap us with false promises of a good life that can never in fact ever really be good. Here is shame. Here is evil.

The richest 1% of the world's population cock-up big-time and cause possibly the worst financial crisis of modern times, and it is we, the 99%, including the poorest and most vulnerable people - people who had absolutely nothing to do with this crisis - who must suffer the cut-backs of 'austerity' and bail out the bastards who caused the cock-up. Notice that they cocked-up because they want to make money - well, take it from others - and good gracious, they're making money now.

We must wonder whether change will ever be possible. If the right sort of change does not occur, we are all in for a massively dismal future - except the very wealthy, of course, who never suffer the privations of the poor, excepting (though less frequently) only illness, and then even a death-bed adorned with the finest and most expensive silks, satins, or cottons, will be of no more use than the shabby and decrepit affair endured by those other straitened souls during their final hours. The question is, what sort of life do we want, or rather, what sort of life are we entitled to, for all those years before the final reckoning befalls us? We all end up at the same place, but it is the laughter of the 1% as on full throttle they scream past the rest of us that leaves a ringing in my ears.

They enjoy their wealth at the expense of privations suffered by others. If this is evil, there is a second evil at work in allowing it to happen.

It has been alleged that those being initiated into the Bullingdon Club - an exclusive society at Oxford University for the sons of the rich elite who preserve their advantages partly through the private education system - must burn a fifty-pound note in front of a tramp after giving the impression that they were about to give the money as a generous gift to ease the woes of homelessness [see *The Daily Mirror*, 23 February 2013]. Government policies are now doing the equivalent of burning a fifty-pound note in front of every poor person, every unemployed person, every sick and disabled person, every day, for day after day after day.

Dear God, we get it.

Our elite rulers, our privileged masters, are stinking rich. They can have what they want, and to get even more they have decided to make us poorer still.

We get it. The regard they have for us, if they have any at all, is the regard an owner has for their slave, and can be distilled down to nothing more than the determination to use us as a productive resource whose purpose is to fuel their greed.

Is it ever right to use physical force in protest against governments and the abuse of power?

When I was a small child and subjected to bullying on the part of cruel and mean classmates and several adults, a child psychologist who was called in to assess the case specifically and unequivocally *instructed* me to respond to violence with violence. If I were hit, I was to strike back. I should aim to defeat my oppressor with the same tool of violence that they were attempting to use against me. They wished to inflict pain and humiliation, and I was told to wish it back upon *them*. Is this a fair model for how we should respond to the oppression of the capitalist System? Will they listen to us if we do *not* respond in this way? What would be the point? What did the riots that inspired us to write this book really achieve? Is the oppression of the System lessening? Are humane ideals directing political policies? Does our welfare count any more than it did before? Of course not.

People should stop defining themselves and others in terms of their work. When you are asked 'What do you do?' say 'I care about the environment,' 'I investigate history,' 'I make music,' 'I read poetry,' 'I am a friend,' or 'I deplore the folly of the world.' Or rather, say something that tells people what you are, not what you do.

Can there be an Alternative Ending? Is there, lurking some-where in the mysteries of Reality, an option we can activate which will unwind all the evil of the modern world and pro-pel us into an alternative universe where what matters is the flourishing of the individual and the proper stewardship of the natural world? Well, of course not. We are stuck with the dismal ending that we are actually experiencing, right now, right here. And this is not the ending we want, and it is not the ending we are prepared to tolerate. So we must change the ending, and bend it from horror and nastiness to make it connect with justice and decency. We must find a way of getting psychopaths out of government and out of all roles that can affect the people they currently dominate. We must find a way to bring morality and value into human affairs and put an end to materialism and consumerism and all the -isms whose functions are really to keep power and money exclusively in the hands of the rich. We want people to feel that vile nastiness of the principle that someone can truly deserve to have double the income of someone else - let alone ten times, a hundred times, or thousands of times the income of the poorest. We want an ending where it doesn't even make sense to talk of 'rich' and 'poor', in which talk of the poorest person rouses a natural revulsion and disgust at the very idea that anyone could willingly create and preside over a System that requires the use of these terms for an ac-count to be made of it. This evil must be brought to an end.

MAKING IT WITHOUT THE MASTERS

The efficient way to total fitness.

Acknowledgements & Sources

The photograph on the front cover is 'Migrant Mother', taken in Nipomo, California in March 1936 by Dorothea Lange (1895-1965), sourced from the Library of Congress < www.loc.gov/rr/print/list/128_migm.html >. This is one of Lange's most iconic images of the Great Depression, and shows Florence Owens Thompson (1903-1983) with her children. Between 1935 and 1939, together with her economist husband Paul Schuster Taylor, Lange documented rural poverty and the exploitation of sharecroppers and migrant labourers, she taking photographs and he recording economic data. Lange distributed her photographs free to newspapers across the United States, bringing to public attention the plight of the dispossessed, downtrodden and exploited. To this day, her poignant images remain icons of the Depression era. Lange remarked of this photograph:

> I saw and approached the hungry and desperate mother, as if drawn by a magnet. I do not remember how I explained my presence or my camera to her, but I do remember she asked me no questions. I made five exposures, working closer and closer from the same direction. I did not ask her name or her history. She told me her age, that she was thirty-two. She said that they had been living on frozen vegetables from the surrounding fields, and birds that the children killed. She had just sold the tires from her car to buy food. There she sat in that lean-to tent

with her children huddled around her, and seemed to know that my pictures might help her, and so she helped me. There was a sort of equality about it.

(*Popular Photography*, February 1960)

The linocut frontispiece by Alfred Lippincott from < occupydesign.org > is licensed under the Creative Commons Attribution-ShareAlike 3.0 Unported License. The goal of Occupy Design 'is to create freely available visual tools around a common graphic language to unite the 99%. The project places an emphasis on producing infographics and icons to improve the communication of the movement's messages and the data surrounding them across the world.' From the same source and under the same licence we have taken the following designs: the raised fist holding a pen on the title page, the quote from Adam Smith opposite the Contents page, the quotation from Plutarch on page 20, and the poster by Alon Raab and Steve Patapoff on page 164.

The photograph by Eric Hossinger facing the Introduction showing a police officer in riot gear at the London student protests (9 December 2010) is a public domain image sourced from Wikimedia Commons < bit.ly/HMbHou > used under the Creative Commons Attribution 2.0 Generic license.

The photograph by Andy Armstrong on the last page of the Introduction showing scenes from the London Riots (8 August 2011) is a public domain image sourced from Wikimedia Commons < bit.ly/1fpRu41 > used under the Creative Commons Attribution 2.0 Generic license.

The photograph on page 26 by Andrea Booher of the truck in a tree after Hurricane Katrina struck New Orleans in 2005 is a public domain image sourced from the FEMA website < 1.usa.gov/1gvbftW >

The diagram showing Maslow's 'Hierarchy of Needs' on page 32 is adapted from several sources, without, we think, reproducing any one source exactly as it appears. Searching for *Maslow's hierarchy of needs* will bring up all the sources we examined, and others.

The picture on page 36 by Benjamin Lloyd entitled *Spooning Yarn, Dallas Cotton Mills, Dallas, Texas, USA* (1865?-1915?) is a public domain image sourced from Wikimedia Commons < bit.ly/1gvayAQ >

The picture by καπιος on page 50, from May 2011, showing Loukanikos the Athens Riot Dog being subjected to police brutality is a public domain image sourced from Wikimedia Commons < bit.ly/1gXL7p1 > and is used under the terms of the Creative Commons Attribution-Share Alike 2.0 Generic license.

The elephant on page 57, photographed in June 2010 by Muhammad Mahdi Karim, is a female African bush elephant in Mikumi National Park, Tanzania. This is a public domain image sourced from Wikimedia Commons < bit.ly/1lByRRo > used under the terms of the GNU Free Documentation License, Version 1.2.

The spoof poster on page 64 entitled 'Keep Calm Conservatives - War on the Poor II' by Byzantine_K is a public domain image sourced from the foter.com website < bit.ly/OOdA8R > used under the terms of the Creative Commons Attribution 2.0 Generic license.

Byzantine_K remarks:

The country - the sick, the disabled, the unemployed, and for that matter most of the workforce that remains employed (with no thanks to the Tories) - have no future if the Conservatives continue in government. Hopefully we will be rid of them by

May 2015, but the damage already caused since 2010 is already considerable.

For many thousands of people it is already too late. Many of the sick and disabled in particular (now well over 10,600) have died having been falsely found 'fit to work' by the corrupt assessment system of the DWP and Atos among others; many of these have committed suicide, many more have suffered physically and mentally as a result of the inhumane practices of this government. Barely a day goes by without a shocking revelation of mistreatment, whether of a dying (and now deceased) blind cancer sufferer, a severely disabled boy being told that he must be assessed for ability to work, and a man with Downs Syndrome being evicted from his home because of cuts - and this within Witney, the constituency of our very own verminous Prime Minister.

Although the spoof Atos Healthcare poster on page 69 appears on the Internet at dozens of locations, we have been unable to track down its creator or its original posting. We must presume that, given its history, it was deliberately put into the public domain as a tool for commentators and activists to highlight and draw attention to the immoralities attending the Conservative government's treatment of disabled people, and the complicit role Atos is playing in perpetrating evil.

To follow up the claim that 10,600 people have died (in 2011) as the direct result of government welfare reforms, see this from the Department for Work and Pensions (the 10,600 statistic appears on the last page) < bit.ly/1gj2bnt > this article on the Work Capability Assessment at Wikipedia < bit.ly/1dFhs4A > and this from Black Triangle Campaign < bit.ly/1ack4pf >

The photograph on page 72 by Craig Sunter taken on 21 October 2012, entitled 'Cogs!', shows the old crane along the Bridgewater canal at Worsley Village, Manchester, UK, and is a public domain image sourced

from Wikimedia Commons < bit.ly/OBOGZa > used under the terms of
the Creative Commons Attribution 2.0 Generic license. This large cog is
entitled to make all the other little cogs move according to its whim in
virtue merely of its massive bulk.

The pie chart and the graph on page 88, showing statistics from the
Department for Work and Pensions, are from the poverty.org.uk website < bit.ly/1lKphsj >

The graph of atmospheric carbon dioxide (prepared by Narayanese,
Sémhur, and the NOAA) and its caption, on page 91, is a public domain
image sourced from Wikimedia Commons < bit.ly/1n5Jxom > used under
the Creative Commons Attribution-Share Alike 3.0 Unported license.

The illustration of the climbers on the mountain on page 95 is made
using clipart images sourced at vector.me < bit.ly/1epX6PQ >

The gearshift diagram on page 96 is a public domain image sourced
from Wikimedia Commons < bit.ly/1ue5pCO >

The spoof UK General Election ballot paper on page 120, showing no alternative to Pro-Capitalism candidates, was created by Karl Gruber, and is in
the public domain. Please contact us for a high-definition jpg or PDF.

The photograph on page 123, taken on 5 November 2011 by Alan Denney
featuring the banner 'Capitalism Isn't Working', shows the secondary
Occupy London camp at Finsbury Square in the City of London, and is a
public domain image sourced from Wikimedia Commons < bit.ly/1l272
hJ > used under the terms of the Creative Commons Attribution 2.0
Generic license.

The Basic Income poster on page 132, from thebasicincome.org.uk website < bit.ly/1kCowOO > is used under the Creative Commons Attribution-ShareAlike 2.0 UK license.

The text of the Universal Declaration of Human Rights in the Appendix on pages 137-46 was sourced from < www.un.org/en/documents/udhr > and is in the public domain.

The Occupy Together poster by Raina Dayne on page 150 is a public domain image sourced from the occupytogether.org website < bit.ly/1g WPo9R > and is used under a Creative Commons license.

www.ingramcontent.com/pod-product-compliance
Lightning Source LLC
Chambersburg PA
CBHW032015170526
45157CB00002B/705